EDGAR'S MISSION
a farm sanctuary | our mission is kindness

Edgar's Mission is a not-for-profit farm sanctuary that seeks to create a humane and just world for all. The sanctuary is set on 153 peaceable acres outside Lancefield, nestled in the tranquillity of the Macedon Ranges, and provides a safe haven for over 450 rescued animals.

Pam Ahern is the founder and director of Edgar's Mission and dedicates her life to the protection of farmed animals. She is the Australian World Animal Day Ambassador. Since 2003, thousands of farmed animals have been given a second chance at life after making their way through the gates of Edgar's Mission.

edgarsmission.org.au

EDGAR'S MISSION

COOKING WITH
KINDNESS

Over 70 recipes from Australia's best vegan chefs and restaurants

PHOTOGRAPHY BY
JULIE RENOUF

COLLECTED BY PAM AHERN

Affirm press

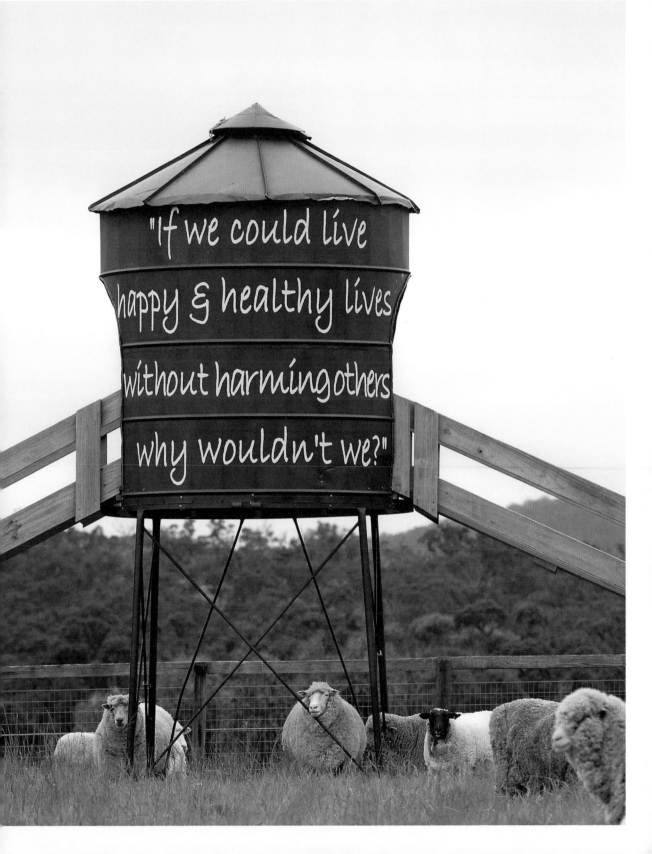

CONTENTS

Marieke, Pam and Teresa at a Women of Letters event

FOREWORD
Marieke Hardy

I'd like to say that my vegan journey started with a pig. But it didn't really. It started because I *was* a pig.

Allow me to elaborate.

I have always enjoyed a lavishly hedonistic relationship with food. As an awkward child, I bullied my peers into Blyton-inspired midnight feasts of thickly buttered sandwiches and chocolate biscuits, all inhaled by torchlight. At teenage parties I hovered next to the food table, often laden with salty, flaky pastries liberally dabbed with tomato sauce while the more confident pals daringly gyrated to Living Colour.

In the early 2000s – after I graduated from the sorts of chaotic, cheery potluck dinners of misspent youth – I started getting into quite serious eating, and eating well. I gravitated towards the types of people who might be halfway through a meal when they started dreaming about tomorrow's lunch, or who considered buying special things on the way home for an in-between taste, or who loved nothing more than regaling others with a romantic sonnet of a fondly remembered gastronomic occasion. I read the food poetry of the peerless M.F.K Fisher. With a group of friends I even fashioned a 'highbrow Dining Club', which involved us dressing up in costume and gorging ourselves to eye-rolling stupidity at fancy degustations throughout Melbourne.

Food was a total joy and pleasure in my life and I fancied myself quite the sophisticate as I lunged from charcuterie board to crème brûlée, occasionally pausing to wipe crumbs from my lap.

Perhaps it goes without saying that I was also an animal lover, because honestly, who isn't? How often do you hear someone loudly proclaiming, 'If there's one thing I just cannot stand it is those blasted animals'? Certainly there are the traditional dog-people-versus-cat-people wars, and various types of serious allergies, along with possibly rational fears that result from past traumatic experiences (a horse stood on my wrist when I was five, breaking it, and I've since afforded the entire species the sort of solemn, timid respect usually shown to members of the monarchy during a street parade). But for the most part, nearly all of us will melt at a video of a pig befriending a duck, or a border collie in a Santa hat, or turtles making love to a Barry White soundtrack.

By 2008, you could say I loved food and I loved animals. While I occasionally glimpsed gory videos on my social media pages of factory farming, and the meat industry made me shriek and reach urgently for the off button, there was still an emotional disconnect. I didn't want to think about where the six-course slow-cooked simmered-in-jus plates were coming from before they were delicately placed in front of me.

And that's when I met Lindsay.

Lindsay 'The Doctor' McDougall was a funny, warm, kind, sharply clever vegan who I was invited to pretend to be friends with on Triple J's breakfast radio five days a week. We were forced together like shy strangers in the mysterious arranged marriage kind of contract that constitutes a 'radio team'. Thankfully, I enjoyed his company instantly. He presented me with an alternative perspective on a 'vegan lifestyle' outside of my blinkered, cynical suspicions (excessive broccoli, yoga pants as outdoor wear, Ben Harper records). Lindsay ate what looked to be very, very delicious food (I was always interested in what he ate; I was interested in what *everybody* ate), he laughed a lot, he talked about eating almost as much as I did. When I wasn't filling three hours of airtime with him every morning talking absolute bunkum, I just wanted to hug his face a great deal.

And then he dared me to go vegan.

'For a week,' he stated. 'End of October. To coincide with World Vegan Day. You love animals and every time you see a dog on the street you practically harass it and it's time for you to start connecting what you put in your mouth with all the love you have in your heart for the voiceless who need our help.'

There was a long pause while I considered this startling prospect. I deeply admired my pocket-sized friend.

'But what, Lindsay …' I responded, rather pathetically, 'about cheese?'

October 2017 will mark my nine-year veganniversary (reader, I never, ever went back). Less than a year after my dear Lindsay threw down the vegan dare as though challenging me to a dance-off battle on a rap mat, I was sent to Edgar's Mission for a photoshoot and experienced the life-changing fortune of meeting Heart Warrior Pam Ahearn. Pam inspired me (alongside writer Michaela McGuire) to start Women of Letters, a spoken word event that raises money specifically for Edgar's Mission. And as Women of Letters toured the world and released seven books (and counting), gently raising awareness for our animal friends, I experienced further lights-on moments about animal advocacy and welfare and experienced what it is like to push through the world with a kind agenda.

But I digress. We were talking about food.

In the last nine years I have sought out fine dining vegan restaurants in Paris, stumbled upon a raw vegan cafe in the middle of Reykjavik, made new friends in wholefoods stores in Croatia bathed in the heady aromas of garlic and spices, and tasted sticky tempeh whilst looking across the rice paddies of Ubud. I ate Isa Moskowitz's swanky vegan comfort food at her Modern Love restaurant in Brooklyn and hugged her until I cried. I'm vegan, and I still think about food all the time, and what I just ate, and what I might eat next, and what I might now share with whom. It's a wonderful hobby, a side project if you will, and a privileged escape.

The most important thing of all is that I have connected what I put in my mouth with the voiceless animals. And I want to invite people in. I want to reassure you all that a vegan dining life is still rich and ludicrous and connective and heartfelt and sexy. I'm still enjoying three-hour dinners that end with everyone having one last sip of brandy and groaning happily on the way home in the back seat of a taxi. Except now I do that heartfully, mindfully, openly, and supportively love our animal friends and comrades and companions.

I could have written this introduction with lots of facts about animal rights and the positive environmental impacts of a vegan diet but I must be utterly honest with you. I am, and always have been, a total pig. And thank god for that, because through Pam and Edgar's Mission I now get to be a friend of pigs too.

Marieke Hardy

A RECIPE FOR KINDNESS

*Pam Ahern,
founder and director of Edgar's Mission*

For as long as I can remember, I have been captivated by animals.

I was just seven years old when the scent of freshly wrapped presents led me into my parents' bedroom. Mum's words 'Don't go behind my dresser' were enough to tell this intrepid young sleuth exactly where she had stashed the Christmas gifts intended for my sister and me. Carefully unwrapping each little package, my heart beat faster and faster when the animal figurines emerged, as I knew our futures would be entwined come 25 December. I wished to linger longer, but realised if I did, the chances of that shared future not happening would be exponentially increased! So, I rewrapped the curios, retracing the original paper folds and sticky tape lines perfectly — well, as perfectly as any overexcited child could. Curiosity sated, I made my way back to the kitchen, downed a ham sandwich and large glass of milk, and resumed playing with my toy animal farm set, dreaming of the new additions that I would soon welcome.

It would take me another few decades before I connected the choices I made in my life and the impact they had on the lives of the animals I professed to love.

My first animal friends were family pets Blackie and Tiny, two diametrically opposed cats, and our goofy and loveable labrador, Laddie, and the bees in our backyard that I would feverishly follow around for hours as they fluttered from flower to flower. I was the kid who attracted the neighbourhood stray animals, fostering many lost and abandoned cats and dogs, so it's no surprise that I went on to found the Central Highland Animal Shelter with my mother as my accomplice. We would take in all the strays from three local pounds — animals who would otherwise have been killed — and at our own expense have the animals vet checked, immunised and desexed, then rehomed if at all possible. This was in the days before the internet, before we had social media and crowd funding to aid our cause.

Around this time, I started looking for more ways to help animals and a newspaper article caught my eye, about companies that did not test their household products and cosmetics on animals. Seeing how others were making a difference spurred me on, and springboarded me to an anti-fur rally in Melbourne. I look back and see shy Pam standing on the periphery in her woollen skirt and leather belt, eagerly listening to the many conversations that were buzzing around. I was introduced to a book called *Animal Liberation* by Peter Singer, and despite its somewhat daunting name, I was curious. After all, it did have the word 'animal' in the title.

I wasn't too far into the book before Peter Singer claimed me as another convert. His perplexed attitude after being served ham sandwiches by a chapter of the RSPCA really struck a chord with me. The principles of honesty, justice and credibility were values that had been instilled in me from a very young age and I thought, *How can I tell people I care deeply about animals while eating them, and then expect to be taken seriously?* From that point on, my life and my menu changed forever.

Overnight I became a 'vedge-ann', as I announced to my mother the next morning. There would be no more meat, dairy or eggs for us. Now, that was pretty radical at the time, especially in the small country town of Woodend. The only non-dairy milk available came in a box, powdered stuff that you mixed up with water. It tasted absolutely disgusting. Mum and I raced out and bought tofu because that's what we thought vedge-anns ate, and it, too, was disgusting. Mind you, we ate it raw! That's how isolated I was.

The thought of a lettuce-leaf-and-alfalfa diet never really cut it for me but back then, it seemed there was no road map for gastronomic salvation with compassion.

Even though I thought I was going to starve, there was no going back, because I had finally made that vital connection between my choices and their effect on the lives of the animals I loved. And, luckily,

Edgar, Pam and Chicquin *(Photo credit: Chris Beck)*

I was only a vedge-ann for a short while before I ran into a kindly vegan who politely corrected my pronunciation.

Soon enough, I found myself on the doorstep of Animals Australia and their 'Save Babe' campaign. It was 2003 and the Code of Practice for Pig Farming was up for review. One of the many things that I believe makes Australia so great is that legislation can be changed to reflect new ways of thinking, as we gain better knowledge and our thoughts evolve. In short, this review represented a golden opportunity to change our flawed animal protection laws, and the campaign would ultimately prove successful in making certain practices no longer legal.

As luck would have it, James Cromwell, who played Farmer Hoggett in the hit movie *Babe*, was in Australia at the time and readily accepted our request to help the very animals who helped to earn him an Oscar nomination. But what we really needed was a pig for a photoshoot. We approached a children's farm and they said yes, but using one of their pigs would cost $150. 'Pigs!' I uttered as I set forth to procure myself a pig. And procure one poop-covered piglet I did. I called him Edgar Alan Pig.

My first task was to get Edgar accustomed to walking on a lead and being around people, so off we went to the local park, my pig on one side and my little dog, ET, on the other. People came from everywhere, curious to see a pig up close. Edgar, in all his porcine glory, proved to be a stellar ambassador for his kind. Watching people's interactions with Edgar made me realise that the best way to change people's view of farmed animals was to introduce them to the animals themselves. While I could talk to people's minds, Edgar grunted eloquently straight to their hearts.

Those were the first trotter steps towards establishing Edgar's Mission, as I laid plans to create a sanctuary to provide a safe haven for as many farmed animals as could be rescued and a voice for those who could not. Today Edgar's Mission gives hope to farmed animals everywhere and those who care for them.

But we are not the only beacon of hope as more and more people are waking up to a kinder way of living, one that is gentler to our minds, better for our health, kinder to animals and more in sync with the planet. More and more restaurants are offering vegan options, more and more people are taking to cruelty free cooking, and more and more are savouring the delights of this kindness as they come to realise the power to create a kinder world is as close as their plate. With all of this in mind, a ladle of pride in my heart and lots of delicious taste testings in my belly, I give thanks to the amazing chefs who have so generously shared their recipes in our first cookbook, *Cooking with Kindness*.

Now, you may wonder why there are no recipes in this book from me. I have to be honest, my signature dish is baked beans on toast (praying all the while that the smoke detector is working). So this book is as much for me as it is for you. There are recipes for beginners as well as culinary treats for highly evolved vegan home cooks.

Bon appetite with a dollop of kindness, on behalf of the many animals' lives you will save.

Pam Ahern

Polly, Pam and Ruby

ABOUT THE RECIPES

To help spread our message of kindness, we invited the chefs of vegan and vegan-friendly cafes and restaurants around Australia to share their recipes for cruelty free cooking in our Edgar's Mission cookbook. We think this is a great way to show that we all have the power to create a kinder world, simply by starting with what's on our plates.

Because these recipes have come from fifty different sources, there are many different styles of recipe writing. Some chefs are cook-how-you-feel geniuses; others are kitchen precision maestros, and we have respected their individual styles. One challenge for some of our kind chefs was to adjust quantities in commercial recipes for cooking at home. Please remember there's a bit of leeway with the serving sizes.

We've included notes on the recipes where the chefs have shared their preferences for brands, as well as handy tips. Some of the ingredients might be unfamiliar to you – if they can't be found in the supermarket health foods aisle, they can usually be sourced at health food shops. One of Edgar's Mission's best friends is The Cruelty Free Shop, Australia's favourite purveyor of everything vegan. Visit their stores in Melbourne, Sydney, Brisbane and Canberra, or shop online: crueltyfreeshop.com.au

We encourage you to jump in and enjoy making these recipes ... and if you don't want to weigh your herbs, we won't tell!

NOTES

AQUAFABA: The liquid in which beans or chickpeas have been cooked has emulsifying and foaming properties, making it an excellent substitute for egg whites.

COCONUT PRODUCTS: Coconut syrup, coconut milk, coconut butter, creamed coconut, coconut oil, coconut sugar, coconut ice-cream, coconut yoghurt – make yourself familiar with the range of products available and you'll never think about dairy products again.

DAIRY: Wherever butter, cheese, cream, ice-cream, yoghurt or other dairy products are mentioned, the intention in the recipe is that they are the dairy-free alternatives.

EGG REPLACER: If you're new to vegan cooking, you might not have noticed that this handy product is now in most supermarkets. Follow the instructions on the packet to veganise some of your old favourite desserts.

FOOD PROCESSORS AND BLENDERS: As a general guide, food processors are good for chopping ingredients finely, but easily overwork things and aren't the best for smooth purees. Blenders are best for smoothness. Stick blenders don't usually get things as smooth as jug blenders, but are good for chopping small quantities of ingredients (e.g. herb pastes) that might get lost in a big food processor.

MEASUREMENTS: You will see some variation in the way cooks measure ingredients in these recipes. Some prefer weight (for accuracy) where others use general quantities like 'handful' or 'a splash'. Some cooks gave us weights as well as cup conversions, to cover all bases. Take this variation in style as a sign that there are no hard and fast rules when it comes to cooking.

NUTRITIONAL YEAST: This inactive yeast is a great source of protein and B vitamins and makes things taste cheesy.

STOCK CUBES: Massel products are vegan, and also free from common food allergens like gluten, lactose, artificial additives and preservatives.

TAHINI: This sesame seed paste can be made from roasted or raw seeds with skins intact (unhulled) or removed (hulled). Most supermarkets stock one or two varieties and health-food stores usually have a complete range.

TOFU: While most supermarkets now stock a range of tofu products, it's in Asian food stores that you'll find the greatest variety, including firm and semi-firm, fried firm, silken.

VEGAN PUFF PASTRY: Nearly all frozen puff pastry is vegan – check the ingredients

BREAKFAST

savoury

sweet

cooked

raw

CHIA SUNRISE

SERVES 2–4

1/4 cup frozen blueberries

1/4 cup frozen strawberries

1 ripe banana (preferably frozen)

2 cups oat milk

1/4 cup rolled oats

1 tablespoon amaranth flakes, optional

1 tablespoon chia seeds

A fast breakfast can still be healthy! This morning smoothie makes for a quick on-the-go breakfast. It can be served in a bowl with your favourite granola for a more substantial meal.

Place the frozen berries in a blender, followed by the banana, then all the other ingredients. Blend until completely smooth.

Note:

AMARANTH FLAKES
can be purchased from
health food stores.

BLACK SMOOTHIE BOWL

SERVES 1–2

1 medium banana

1 1/2 bananas, frozen

1/2 cup crushed ice

1 teaspoon activated charcoal

1/4 cup frozen blueberries

2 medjool dates, pitted

3 tablespoons coconut milk (or more to reach your desired consistency)

granola, coconut flakes, fruit, to serve

Our wholesome nutritious food is made from scratch and tastes delicious, nourishing from the inside out. This is a recipe you must try! It's one of our favourite smoothie bowls, using activated charcoal to boost the nutritional value and act as a natural detoxifier for the body. So get out your blender and try this amazing deep black bowl of goodness.

Add the bananas, ice, charcoal, blueberries, dates and coconut milk to a blender and blend until smooth, stirring as necessary to help the ingredients blend evenly. If it seems too thick, add additional coconut milk.

Once smooth, spoon into a bowl, decorate with your choice of granola, coconut and fruit, and enjoy!

Note:

ACTIVATED CHARCOAL is available from health food stores.

CHOC-BREKKIE GRANOLA

MAKES 250 G

30 g (1/4 cup) sunflower kernels

40 g (1/4 cup) sesame seeds

30 g (1/4 cup) pepitas (pumpkin seeds)

40 g (1/4 cup) activated almonds

45 g (1/4 cup) activated buckwheat

15 g (1/4 cup) coconut chips

25 g (1/4 cup) cranberries

1 quantity date and nut butter

3 squares Pana Chocolate Orange

nut milk, to serve

fresh fruit, to serve

DATE AND NUT BUTTER

1 cup raw nuts of your choice

4 medjool dates, pitted

2 pinches of Himalayan salt

Note:

1 CUP of raw nuts will make 1/2 cup nut butter. Results may vary depending on the nuts you use.

NUT BUTTER can be substituted with tahini for a nut-free alternative.

This is an edited extract from Pana Chocolate, The Recipes *by Pana Barbounis published by Hardie Grant Books, RRP $36, available nationally.*

Granola is an essential breakfast staple (though we nibble on ours at all hours!), and so easy to make. Using our orange chocolate bar in this recipe gives your granola a zesty boost, and means you can get your chocolate hit at any time of day. Play around with tastes and textures – you can mix up the fruits and seeds for added variety. You need a dehydrator for this recipe.

FOR THE BUTTER, blend the nuts in a food processor on high until the oils are released and the mixture resembles butter. Constantly scrape down the sides to ensure even blending. Add the dates, 60 ml (1/4 cup) of filtered water and the salt, then blend again.

Season with a little vanilla, if desired.

FOR THE GRANOLA, combine all dry ingredients in a bowl.

Add some date and nut butter and massage into dry mix. Keep adding butter until all the dry ingredients are coated.

Using a coarse grater or zester, grate the squares of chocolate into the mixture and stir through.

Transfer the mixture to a tray and dehydrate for 8–12 hours.

Once the mixture has been dehydrated, break it into small shards and store in an airtight container until needed.

Serve with nut milk and fresh fruit.

CRUNCHY CITRUS TOASTED GRANOLA

MAKES ABOUT 750 G (8 CUPS)

225 g (2 1/2 cups) rolled oats, rolled barley or rolled triticale (or a combination)

50 g (1 cup) flaked coconut or shredded coconut

70 g (1/2 cup) slivered almonds

50 g (1/3 cup) pumpkin seeds

45 g (1/4 cup) linseeds (flaxseeds)

40 g (1/4 cup) sesame seeds

2 strips each orange, lemon and lime rind, pith removed and shredded

1 tablespoon mixed spice

80 ml (1/3 cup) warmed rice malt syrup or pure maple syrup

50 g melted virgin coconut oil

70 g (1/2 cup) seeded dried dates, chopped

75 g (1/2 cup) dried apricot, sliced

2 dried figs, thinly sliced

coconut or soy yoghurt, citrus segments, nut milk and shredded citrus zest, to serve (optional)

This is an edited extract from Breakfast Bowls *by Caroline Griffiths published by Smith Street Books, RRP $29.99, available in stores nationally. A collection of 52 nourishing recipes, there are many gluten-free options and most recipes are vegan or give tips to make them vegan. They're also refined sugar free.*

A well-balanced breakfast will give your body everything it needs to kickstart your day. Homemade toasted granola (muesli) is so satisfying to make. This recipe makes a big batch and it keeps brilliantly in an airtight container. I love it as the hero of a simple breakfast bowl topped with a splash of nut milk and seasonal fruit, plus a dollop of coconut yoghurt. It is also makes a fantastic crunchy topping for a smoothie bowl or chia pudding.

Preheat the oven to 150°C (130°C fan-forced).

Line 2 baking trays with non-stick baking paper.

Combine the rolled oats and/or the rolled barley and triticale, coconut, almonds, seeds, shredded rind and mixed spice in a large bowl. Add the syrup and melted coconut oil and mix until well combined.

Spread the mixture over the trays, keeping little clumps of mixture together for extra texture. Bake for about 50 minutes, stirring gently after 25 minutes, until just starting to brown.

Remove from the oven and cool on trays (the granola will crisp on cooling). Gently stir in the dried fruit.

To serve, place half a cup of granola in a serving bowl and top with yoghurt, fruit, milk and zest.

Store in an airtight container for 2–3 weeks.

CHICKPEA OMELETTE WITH CORIANDER & LIME DRESSING

SERVES 4

1/2 stalk celery

1/4 carrot

1 dried shiitake mushroom, soaked in warm water for 30 minutes

1 teaspoon chopped ginger

1/2 teaspoon crushed garlic, or to taste

1/4 teaspoon chopped chilli

200 g tempeh

1/4 cup cooked brown rice

1 tablespoon gluten-free soy sauce

1/2 tablespoon sesame seeds

1/2 tablespoon sesame oil

1 tablespoon olive oil, plus extra for frying

small handful of rocket or herbs of your choice

75 g bean shoots

1/8 red cabbage, thinly sliced

BATTER – see next page

DRESSING – see next page

At Straight Up Coffee and Food we are focused on big flavours. This dish not only has bags of flavour, but also great textures, and is visually bright and fresh. Plus it's vegan and gluten free!

FOR THE DRESSING, blend all the ingredients in a blender or with a stick blender for about 2–3 minutes, making sure there are no lumps. Store in an airtight container in the fridge until required.

FOR THE BATTER, blend all the ingredients along with 110 ml water until well combined. Cover with plastic wrap and place in the fridge until required.

FOR THE FILLING, place the celery, carrot, shiitake mushroom, ginger, garlic and chilli in a food processor and blend well for 2–3 minutes. Add the tempeh and pulse 8–9 times until the mixture has a similar texture to rice. Fold through the brown rice.

Scrape the mixture into a mixing bowl, add the soy sauce and sesame seeds, and fold through to combine.

Heat a non-stick frying pan on medium heat, add the sesame and olive oils, and fry the tempeh mixture until golden. Transfer to a bowl, then wipe out the frying pan and return it to the stove on a low heat.

CHICKPEA OMELETTE WITH CORIANDER & LIME DRESSING

CHICKPEA OMELETTE BATTER

170 grams chickpea (besan) flour

230 ml coconut milk

20 ml apple cider vinegar

15 grams vegan miso paste

1/2 teaspoon crushed garlic

1 teaspoon ground turmeric

3/4 teaspoon bicarbonate of soda

CREAMY CORIANDER & LIME DRESSING

225 g silken tofu

1/2 bunch coriander, washed super well

1/8 teaspoon crushed garlic

juice of 1 lime

salt, to taste

FOR THE OMELETTE, add a little oil when the pan is hot, then pour in 3/4 cup chickpea batter, moving the pan to distribute the batter evenly (much like a pancake). Place a lid or tray over the pan and leave the omelette to steam for 1 minute.

Remove the lid and place some of the tempeh mix on half of the omelette. Cover and steam for a further 6 minutes.

Use a spatula to fold the other half of the omelette over the filling and slide out onto a plate. Repeat with remaining batter and fillings.

Serve omelettes with a small salad of rocket, bean shoots and red cabbage and the creamy coriander and lime dressing.

Notes:

LEFTOVER DRESSING will keep in a jar in the fridge for up to 7 days and is amazing on salads and roast potatoes.

THE BATTER will last up to 5 days in the fridge in a sealed container.

VEGAN MISO paste does not contain bonito (dried tuna shavings used in dashi stocks and flavourings) and is available from some supermarkets, health food stores and Asian grocers. Check the label carefully.

HASH BROWNS WITH RAINBOW CHARD, GREEN GODDESS SAUCE & PORTOBELLO MUSHROOMS

SERVES 6

6 portobello mushrooms

olive oil, for cooking

salt and pepper (we use Murray River pink salt flakes)

few sprigs of thyme

1 large bunch rainbow chard

squeeze of lemon juice

sunflower oil, for deep-frying

pea tendrils, to serve

HASH BROWNS

1.2 kg potatoes, approx. (we use Royal Blues)

1 1/2 teaspoons salt, to taste

pinch of freshly ground white pepper

SAUCE – see next page

Our most popular brunch item, these are a game changer to add to your repertoire. They're also my favourite menu item, living up to the stereotype that the Irish love potatoes! This dish is the perfect base – you can change the toppings depending on what's seasonally available. Try it with asparagus, sauteéd snake beans, fennel slaw or whatever tickles your fancy. I came up with a vegan version of our green goddess sauce especially for this book, so I hope you enjoy it as much as we did sampling it!

TO PREPARE THE HASH BROWNS, preheat the oven to 170°C.

Place the potatoes on a baking tray and bake for about 45–50 minutes, or until just slightly undercooked (you want them to be firm enough to hold their shape when grated). Remove from the oven and leave to cool for half an hour.

Grate the potatoes on the largest side of a box grater until you have just skin left. Place the grated potato in a large bowl, add the salt and pepper and mix thoroughly.

Line a tray with baking paper. Scoop the grated potato into a ¼-cup measure, squash it down firmly until it's level with the top and then tap out onto the tray. Repeat until you have 18 discs, dipping the measuring cup in a bowl of water in between to prevent potato sticking to the sides. Place in the fridge to firm up (at least 1–2 hours or overnight).

HASH BROWNS WITH RAINBOW CHARD, GREEN GODDESS SAUCE & PORTOBELLO MUSHROOMS

GREEN GODDESS SAUCE

15 g parsley leaves

15 g chives

10 g mint leaves

10 g tarragon leaves

15 g Dijon mustard

1 small clove garlic

15 ml lemon juice

120 ml soy milk

1/2 teaspoon salt, or to taste

pinch of freshly ground white pepper

130 ml mild olive oil

20 g thick coconut yoghurt, optional

Notes:

ROYAL BLUE potatoes have great flavour and texture – not too floury and not too waxy.

LEFTOVER GREEN GODDESS SAUCE is delicious as a sandwich spread, salad dressing, condiment for platters and myriad other things. Use it to your heart's desire!

THE POTATO SKINS can be fried or baked for use in another dish. If doing this, leave a little flesh on the skins, to hold them together.

FOR THE GREEN GODDESS SAUCE, place everything except the olive oil and coconut yoghurt into the bowl attachment of a stick blender. Blend until the herbs are chopped, then start adding the oil in a slow steady stream until it's emulsified and the herbs are finely blitzed. Add the yoghurt, if using, and mix with a spoon. Refrigerate or set aside until required.

When you are nearly ready to eat, preheat the oven to 180°C.

Place the whole portobello mushrooms gill-side up on a baking tray and drizzle with a little olive oil. Season with salt and pepper and top with sprigs of thyme. Bake for 15 minutes or until cooked. Set aside.

Wash the rainbow chard and dry well. Chop the stalks finely and cut the leaves into 3 cm strips. Drizzle a little olive oil in a hot frying pan, add the rainbow chard and sauté until the stems are tender and the leaves are just starting to wilt. Season with salt and pepper and remove from the heat. Squeeze a little lemon juice in to halt the cooking and brighten the taste of the greens.

Heat enough sunflower oil for deep-frying to 175°C in a large, deep saucepan or deep-fryer. Fry the hash browns until golden and crisp (about 4 minutes) then transfer to a tray or bowl lined with paper towel to drain.

Spoon 1–2 tablespoons of green goddess sauce onto each plate, slightly off centre. Place three hash browns in the centre of each plate and top with sautéed rainbow chard. Arrange a portobello mushroom on top and garnish with pea tendrils.

'COURAGE IS WHAT IT TAKES TO STAND UP AND SPEAK. COURAGE IS ALSO WHAT IT TAKES TO SIT DOWN AND LISTEN.'

Unknown

CURRY & CORIANDER SCRAMBLE ON RYE SOURDOUGH

SERVES 1–2

2 slices rye sourdough

1/4 cup water

150 g organic firm tofu

1 tablespoon tamari or soy sauce

2 tablespoons nutritional yeast

1/2 teaspoon curry powder

handful of coriander, roughly chopped

I used to think people were bonkers for trying to replicate scrambled eggs but it turns out they weren't. And like many people who transition to a plant-based diet, I was not a tofu fan by any stretch of the imagination. Now I can say this has become my favourite vegan breakfast recipe. If you have never had scrambled tofu, do yourself a favour and try it!

Toast the sourdough.

Bring the water to the boil in a non-stick frying pan. Turn the heat down to a simmer and crumble the tofu into the pan. Cook gently until the tofu is heated through and almost all the water has gone.

Add the tamari, nutritional yeast and curry powder. Stir until everything is well combined and continue cooking on a low flame until you get the texture you want.

Check the seasoning. Mix the coriander through and serve with the toasted sourdough.

Notes:

NUTRITIONAL YEAST is an inactive yeast that makes things taste cheesy. You can find it in health food stores.

SCRAMBLE WET OR DRY?
If you prefer your scramble to have a drier texture, just continue cooking for another minute or so.

FOR A SUPER SCRAMBLE
add some chopped roasted potatoes, cherry roma tomatoes and fresh spinach. It also works beautifully with baked beans, mushrooms and vegie sausages.

SERVES 4–6

vegetable oil, for frying

20 mushrooms, sliced

20 cherry tomatoes

4 handfuls of spinach

DOSA BATTER

3 cups (450 g) self-raising flour

2 2/3 cups (660 ml) soy milk, plus extra to adjust consistency, if needed

2 teaspoons sugar

1/3 teaspoon salt

FILLING

8 small white potatoes, washed

2 yellow onions, chopped

4 cloves garlic, minced

1/4 cup olive oil

4 sprigs curry leaves

2 teaspoons ground turmeric

2 teaspoons curry powder

2 pinches of chilli flakes

salt and pepper

SRI LANKAN FARMER'S BREAKFAST

Masala dosa has been a staple in Lentil as Anything's restaurants, and head chef Dipesh from Abbotsford gives his take on the spiced potato-stuffed Sri Lankan crepe. Set yourself up for the day in style with big, warm flavours and the right balance of carbohydrate, protein and vegetables.

TO MAKE THE FILLING, boil the potatoes in a saucepan of water until soft, then drain and mash.

In a frying pan, sauté the onion and garlic in the olive oil. Add the curry leaves and remaining spices, allowing them to cook for a few minutes. Add the mashed potato and mix, then take off the heat. Season with salt and pepper to taste.

FOR THE DOSA BATTER, mix all the ingredients in a bowl until a smooth, runny consistency, just a bit thinner than pancake batter, is achieved, adding more soy milk if needed.

TO COOK THE DOSA, heat 1–2 tablespoons of oil in a frying pan. Pour in a quarter of the batter and cook each side until golden brown. Cover half the pancake with a quarter of the potato mix, then fold to enclose. Remove the pancake from the frying pan, and repeat with remaining batter and filling.

Heat 1–2 tablespoons of oil in a frying pan. Sauté the mushrooms, tomatoes and spinach, and serve alongside the dosa. Enjoy!

SERVES 6

1 small red onion

olive oil spray

1 large corn cob

350 g gluten-free self-raising flour

500 ml soy milk

1 teaspoon sweet paprika, plus extra to serve

200 g creamed corn

1/4 bunch parsley, chopped

100 g cooked corn kernels

pinch of salt

6 spoonfuls smashed avocado

2 long red chillies

1–2 oxheart tomatoes, sliced

1 Black Russian tomato, sliced

20 heirloom cherry tomatoes, cut in half

thinly sliced spring onion, to serve

micro radish, to serve

handful of popped corn, to serve

DRESSING – see next page

MEDICINAL MEXICAN WAFFLES

We have a simple way of deciding whether to include a dish on the Serotonin menu: does it make you happy? In the case of these Medicinal Mexican waffles, the answer is a resounding yes! They look amazing, taste amazing and, even better, pack an incredible amount of plant-powered nutrition to make you feel amazing.

FOR THE DRESSING, place all the ingredients in a blender and process until smooth.

FOR THE VEGIES, preheat a non-stick frying pan over medium–high heat. Cut the onion into 1 cm wedges, keeping the base intact to ensure the layers stay together. Spray the frying pan with olive oil spray and cook the onion wedges until lightly charred.

While the onion is cooking, bring a large saucepan of water to the boil, add the corn cob and boil for 3 minutes. Cut 6 slices off the cob when cool enough to handle, and set aside.

FOR THE WAFFLES, process the flour, soy milk, paprika and creamed corn in a food processor until smooth. Stir in the chopped parsley, corn kernels and salt.

Spoon 1/6 (about 200 g) of the mixture into the waffle machine and cook until golden brown. Repeat with remaining mixture. If your machine is not automatic or self-timing, check every few minutes to ensure waffles do not burn.

MEDICINAL MEXICAN WAFFLES

DRESSING

250 ml crushed tomatillos

2 long red chillies

3 coriander roots, washed

2 cloves garlic

50 ml olive oil

20 ml lemon juice

salt, to taste

We love to plate up so you can see all the colours. To do so, cut each waffle in half, place it in the centre of the plate and arrange the other half on top. Put a spoonful of smashed avocado in the middle and spread the red chilli around it.

Arrange slices of tomato, cherry tomato halves and wedges of charred red onion around the smashed avocado. Sprinkle with the spring onion and micro radish, wedge one of the corn cob slices on top, and finish with the popcorn and a dusting of paprika.

Opposite: Kyle Behrend with Ruby and the
Kindness Burger

BANANA PANCAKES WITH BERRIES

MAKES 12 PANCAKES

4 ripe bananas, mashed

1 teaspoon cinnamon

1 teaspoon pure vanilla essence

4 cups self-raising flour

4 cups soy milk, plus extra to adjust consistency, if needed

vegetable oil, for frying

maple syrup, to serve

coconut milk ice-cream, to serve

icing sugar, to serve

mint leaves, to serve (optional)

BERRY COMPOTE

500 g frozen berries (we use strawberries and blueberries)

Note:

LEFTOVER BERRY COMPOTE will keep in the fridge in an airtight container for up to 5 days and makes a delicious topping for all kinds of breakfasts.

Wombat Cafe's initial menu was put together without a whole lot of prior planning. I simply made a list of things that I liked, were easy to prepare and that I hoped would appeal to a broad range of tastebuds. I make these for my nephew Cooper who's one of the fussiest eaters of all time. The pancakes have developed a cult following in the cafe and are one of our most Instagrammed items. They're super easy and quick to prepare.

To make the compote, place the frozen berries in a saucepan and cook over low heat until heated through and softened. Simple!

For the pancakes, combine the mashed banana, cinnamon, vanilla and flour in a large bowl. Pour in the soy milk, mixing thoroughly and adding extra if required until the batter is thin enough to ladle.

In an oiled frying pan (or flat hotplate) on medium heat, cook ladlefuls of batter until bubbles appear on the surface, then flip over. Remove when lightly browned on both sides.

Stack pancakes on serving plates and top with berry compote, a swirl of maple syrup and a scoop of coconut milk ice-cream. Dust with icing sugar, garnish with mint leaves and serve.

CHIA COCONUT PUDDING WITH FRESH MANGO MOUSSE

SERVES 2–4

1 x 400 ml can coconut milk

1 cup rice milk, almond milk or water

1 teaspoon vanilla extract

1/3–1/2 cup chia seeds

2 tablespoons maple syrup

pinch of cinnamon or nutmeg, or 1 teaspoon rosewater, optional

2 ripe mangoes, flesh removed

juice and zest of 1 lime

coconut flakes, to serve

finely chopped mint, to serve, optional

Are you bored with your toast or muesli breakfast, or just want to try something different? This delightful chia pudding is a great healthy breakfast recipe to have up your sleeve. It will keep in the fridge for 2–3 days, ready to go in the morning, and you can adjust the topping to suit the season, or what you've got at hand.

To make the chia pudding, mix together the coconut milk, rice milk, vanilla, chia seeds, maple syrup and spices or rosewater, if using, and allow to stand for 5 minutes. Stir again, cover and place in the fridge for about 3 hours, or overnight. (You can eat the pudding after about 45 minutes if you are short on time.)

Roast the coconut flakes in a heavy-based frying pan over medium heat, without any extra oil, until a light golden colour. This only takes a few minutes and you should keep a close watch as the coconut can burn very quickly! Set aside.

To make the topping, blend the mango in a blender, hand-held mixer or small food processor to a mousse-like texture with a little lime juice (or chop finely and dress with lime juice, if you prefer).

Spoon a layer of pudding into serving glasses, followed by the mango topping, and garnish with toasted coconut flakes, a touch of lime zest, and mint, if using.

Notes:

CHIA SEEDS QUANTITY can be varied, depending on whether you prefer the pudding slightly thicker or lighter.

CHANGE THE FRUIT TOPPING to chopped apple, pear or papaya, or stewed rhubarb and strawberries.

WALNUTS OR MACADAMIAS can be used instead of coconut flakes.

INCA BERRIES (dried Cape gooseberries), goji berries or prunes can be added to the pudding mixture.

ANNA WEATHERLAKE
Animal rights advocate

&

PETER SIDDLE
Australian cricketer

I have never understood why people love some animals, yet eat others. I was raised as a vegetarian and transitioned to veganism in 2011. It was a natural progression for me and I switched almost overnight after discovering the truth about the dairy industry after watching the Earthlings documentary. I could no longer sit back and say I didn't know about the cruelty behind it, and therefore I could no longer support that industry by purchasing dairy products. My husband, Peter Siddle, followed soon after, first trying vegetarianism before transitioning to a full vegan diet within three months. We have both thrived on a vegan diet and would not have it any other way.

So why are Sids and I vegan? There are many reasons. Firstly, we are vegan for the animals. Knowing we can live and thrive off a plant-based diet that causes no harm to animals makes it a no-brainer for us. We feel much healthier and happier living a vegan lifestyle and we both believe our health is better than it has ever been since making the change. Secondly, we are firm believers in being as kind to the environment as possible.

Animal agriculture is the leading cause of habitat destruction, species extinction, ocean dead zones and water pollution and we take great comfort in knowing that we are not contributing to that by keeping animals off our plates.

Being vegan has never been a challenge for us. We believe that consuming a vegan diet is only as hard as you make it. When you put your own health, the animals' welfare and our environment first, rather

Peter and Anna with mum, Carol, and Cookie and Kris Kringle

than dwelling on whether things are harder or not, veganism comes naturally. Both Sids and I travel quite regularly in Australia and abroad for his work and we have never felt limited in terms of choice when dining out. Most restaurants these days offer vegan and vegetarian options and some of Melbourne's top restaurants such as Maha, Morris Jones and Attica offer vegan menus as well. We also like to ensure we are well prepared, travelling with a small blender wherever we go so we can maintain our home routine of making smoothies.

Sids' transition to veganism has been interesting for me to observe. Not only has his transformation been incredible, I've greatly admired the way he's handled a lot of (unwarranted) criticism. People believe that you need meat and dairy to be a staple part of your diet when you're an elite athlete. However, this is not the case at all. As a result of changing his diet, Sids' recovery time after games has shortened, and he is leaner, stronger and fitter than he has ever been. In fact, he now believes that he has prolonged his playing career simply by making kinder and healthier food choices.

We are proud to live a lifestyle that causes as little harm to animals and the environment as possible, and we hope to encourage others to do the same.

www.earthbyanna.com

SNACKS

savoury

cooked

raw

HOMEMADE HUMMUS

MAKES 1.5 CUPS

1/4 cup tahini

1 large lemon, squeezed

2 tablespoons olive oil

1/2 teaspoon ground cumin

pinch of salt

1 large clove garlic, minced

1 can chickpeas, rinsed

2 tablespoons water

Here's a great dip that's easy to make. It's a good traveller, making it perfect for picnic spreads and taking your lunch to work. If you're using it in sandwiches or wraps, pack it in a separate reusable container so sogginess is a thing of the past. Have it on hand for healthy snacking with fresh vegies.

Blend tahini and lemon in a food processor for 1 minute.

Add olive oil, cumin, salt and garlic and blend for 30 seconds. Scrape down the sides of the bowl and blend for another 30 seconds.

Add approximately half of the chickpeas to the food processor and blend. Scrape down the sides of the bowl and blend the remaining chickpeas until the consistency is smooth.

Slowly add 1 tablespoon of water at a time, blending until the hummus is the perfect consistency.

Store in the fridge in an airtight container.

CREAMY CHIPOTLE AIOLI

MAKES ABOUT 40 SERVES

200 g cashews, soaked for at least 2 hours in cold water

40 ml flavour-neutral oil (we use rice bran oil)

60 ml lime juice

3 cloves garlic

2 chipotles in adobo

30 g coconut sugar, plus extra to taste, if needed

10 g salt (we use Himalayan salt), plus extra to taste

1–2 teaspoons smoked paprika

One of our most requested recipes ... This silky-smooth, spicy, tangy sauce is so easy to make and pairs well with everything. Our favourite way to enjoy it is as a snack, with handcut chips, but it works a treat on burgers and sandwiches too.

Blend all of the ingredients in a blender until a thick paste forms (if your blender is weak, use a food processor for this step). Gradually add 200 ml water and blend until super smooth and thick. Add extra salt and sugar to taste.

Notes:

CHIPOTLES IN ADOBO are smoked Mexican chillies in a rich spicy sauce. They come in small cans and can be found in the international aisle of most supermarkets.

THE CONSISTENCY can be easily varied. Make this thick, as shown here, to use as a spread, or a thinner sauce by varying the amount of water added.

AIOLI will keep in an airtight container in the fridge for up to 6 days, and also freezes well. Make a big batch of a thicker consistency, freeze half for later and thin down with oil or water as required.

SWEET POTATO CHIPS WITH TOFU AIOLI

SERVES 6–8

6 medium sweet potatoes, cut into wedges (leave the skin on)

coconut oil spray

salt (I use Murray River salt)

pepper

chilli flakes and ground turmeric, optional

TOFU AIOLI

250 g silken tofu

1 clove garlic (or to taste)

1 teaspoon salt

pinch of cayenne pepper

juice of 1/2 a lemon

Handcut sweet potato chips – does it get any better? Only if you eat them with tofu aioli! Seriously, this combo is so yummy it defies belief. Try it and see!

FOR THE TOFU AIOLI, blitz all the ingredients in a high-speed or bullet blender. Store in a sealed container in the fridge until required (it will keep for up to 4 days).

Preheat the oven to 180°C and line a baking tray with baking paper.

Place sweet potato wedges skin-side down on lined tray and bake for approximately 15 minutes, until cooked through but still retaining a little bite (check this with a metal skewer).

Remove from the oven and allow to cool. You can store the wedges in the fridge at this point and finish cooking later.

For the final stage, preheat the oven to 200°C. Place the sweet potatoes on a lined tray, same as before, and spray with coconut oil. Season with salt and pepper, and sprinkle with chilli flakes and turmeric, if using. Roast until GBD – golden brown and delicious – and serve with tofu aioli.

CHEESY RAW ARANCINI BALLS WITH JALAPEÑOS

MAKES 15–20 BALLS

3 large parsnips, peeled and roughly chopped

2 cups cashews

60 ml Bragg All Purpose Seasoning (see note)

1 teaspoon ground turmeric

4 tablespoons nutritional yeast flakes

1/4 cup raw sesame seeds, for coating

pinch of sumac, for coating

lime wedges, to serve

vegan sour cream, to serve

pickled jalapeños, to serve

Notes:

BRAGG ALL PURPOSE SEASONING is a soy sauce alternative made from liquid amino acids and can be found at health food stores. If it is not available use organic tamari instead.

NUTRITIONAL YEAST FLAKES are also known as savoury yeast flakes.

These raw arancini balls are so versatile. Fabulous as finger food at a party, or delicious as an anytime snack, you can even turn them into a meal with a salad on the side. Yum!

Place the parsnips in a food processor and pulse until they take on a rice-like consistency. Don't over-pulse or you will end up with a paste.

Transfer the parsnip 'rice' to a large bowl before processing the cashews, seasoning, turmeric, yeast flakes and 2 tablespoons water until creamy.

Add the cashew mixture to the bowl with the parsnip rice and mix together well with clean hands.

Combine the sesame seeds and sumac (or other spice of your choice) on a large plate.

Shape the arancini mixture into balls approximately 2 cm in diameter, and then roll in the spicy sesame seeds to coat.

Refrigerate for 2 hours before serving.

Serve with lime wedges, vegan sour cream and pickled jalapeños on the side.

CURRIED VEGETABLE SAMOSAS WITH LEMON & MINT DIPPING YOGHURT

MAKES 24 SAMOSAS

1 tablespoon coconut oil

1 clove garlic, crushed

5 cm piece ginger, grated

1/2 cup korma curry paste

1 teaspoon ground cumin

1 teaspoon ground turmeric

1 vegetable stock cube

3 medium potatoes, finely diced

2 carrots, finely diced

1 large zucchini, finely diced

1 sweet potato, finely diced

large handful of chopped coriander

large handful of chopped mint

1 cup frozen peas

6 squares frozen vegan puff pastry, defrosted

vegetable or coconut oil spray

YOGHURT DIPPING SAUCE –
see next page

These little gems were created by my wonderful mum for our first-ever function at Wombat Cafe, which was held before we even opened. They were so popular we decided to include them on our opening menu. They're super easy to prepare and the recipe is very forgiving, so you can't go wrong. You can use whatever veg you have on hand, and let's face it, almost anything cooked in puff pastry tastes pretty good!

FOR THE FILLING, place the coconut oil, garlic, ginger, curry paste and ground spices in a large saucepan and cook for 2–3 minutes until fragrant.

Add 2 cups of water and simmer for a few minutes, then add the stock cube.

Add the potatoes, carrots, zucchini, sweet potato and herbs. Cook until tender, then stir in the peas.

If the mixture is too liquid continue to simmer until it thickens (it will also thicken on cooling). Remove from the heat and allow to cool completely.

Preheat the oven to 220°C.

TO MAKE THE SAMOSAS, cut each pastry sheet into four squares and place a heaped tablespoon of filling in the centre of each square. Gather up all four corners and twist together.

CURRIED VEGETABLE SAMOSAS WITH LEMON & MINT DIPPING YOGHURT

YOGHURT DIPPING SAUCE

1 x 500 g tub natural coconut yoghurt

juice and zest of 2 lemons

handful of finely chopped mint

1/2 cucumber, finely diced

salt and pepper

cucumber slices, to serve

Place the samosas on a baking tray lined with baking paper and spray lightly with oil. Bake in the oven until browned, about 12 minutes.

MAKE THE DIPPING SAUCE while the samosas are baking by combining all the ingredients (minus a small amount of lemon zest for garnishing) in a bowl. Decorate with cucumber slices, sprinkle with lemon zest, and serve with the warm samosas.

Notes:

PREPARE THE FILLING the day before and keep covered in the fridge until ready to use – the flavours will develop and your samosas will be even tastier.

THE DIPPING SAUCE recipe allows a quarter cup to 3 samosas.

'I LIKE PIGS.
DOGS LOOK UP TO US.
CATS LOOK DOWN ON
US. PIGS TREAT US
AS EQUALS.'

Sir Winston Churchill

TOFU SATAY

SERVES 4–6

2 x 400 g blocks firm tofu, fried if available, cut into 2 cm cubes

2–4 tablespoons rice bran oil (or sunflower oil)

TOFU MARINADE

2 cm piece galangal, peeled and chopped (or ginger)

4 stalks lemongrass, inner white part only, thinly sliced

2 cloves garlic, sliced

5 small red shallots or 1 medium red onion, sliced

60 ml sunflower oil

60 g coconut sugar (or brown sugar)

1 teaspoon tamari (or light soy sauce)

1 tablespoon ground turmeric

1 tablespoon ground coriander

1 tablespoon ground cumin

1 teaspoon salt

SATAY SAUCE – see next page

Some days the Woking Amazing kitchen just can't keep up with the demand for our satay skewers. So be warned, your friends and family will be coming back for more! We find you can get easily 4 serves of the tofu skewers out of this, and 6–8 serves of the sauce, so keep some sauce in reserve in the fridge or freezer ready to go again …

Start this recipe a day ahead to marinate the tofu. You can also make the satay sauce ahead of time.

FOR THE TOFU MARINADE, blend all the ingredients together until smooth. Transfer to an airtight container, add the tofu cubes and mix thoroughly. Cover and refrigerate overnight.

FOR THE SATAY SAUCE, place the dried chillies in a small saucepan and just cover with water. Bring to the boil, then simmer over low heat for 2 minutes. Remove from the heat, cover and let it cool down for 15 minutes.

Place the chillies and soaking water, galangal, lemongrass, garlic and shallots in a food processor and process until smooth.

Heat the sunflower oil in a medium heavy-based saucepan over medium heat.

Add the blended spice paste, then cook, stirring continuously to prevent it catching on the bottom, for 8–10 minutes, or until there is very little steam rising from the

TOFU SATAY

SATAY SAUCE

10 long dried red chillies, cut in half and seeds removed

1.5 cm piece galangal, peeled and chopped (if unable to source, replace with ginger)

2 small stalks lemongrass, inner white part only, thinly sliced

4 cloves garlic, sliced

6 red shallots or 2 medium red onions, roughly sliced

100 ml sunflower oil

600 ml coconut milk

1 tablespoon tamarind paste

1 tablespoon lime juice, plus extra to taste

80 g coconut sugar (or brown sugar)

pinch of salt, to taste

125 g smooth peanut butter

200 g raw peanuts, dry-roasted and finely chopped

sauce. At this stage, the oil will have split from the spice paste, caramelising into a lovely dark red and developing a beautiful fragrance.

Add the coconut milk and gently bring to the boil. Add the tamarind, lime, sugar, salt, peanut butter and half the chopped peanuts. Gently bring to the boil again, then remove from the heat and set aside until required. Store in the fridge if you are making the sauce the day before.

FOR THE TOFU SKEWERS, thread the tofu cubes onto skewers and grill over a barbecue or in a hot frying pan brushed with rice bran oil for a few minutes on each side.

Just before serving, reheat the satay sauce over low heat, if necessary, and stir in the remaining peanuts. Add more lime juice and salt to taste and serve with the hot tofu skewers.

Notes:

TAMARI is a wheat-free Japanese soy sauce, available in most supermarkets.

LEFTOVER SATAY SAUCE is a winner with grilled vegies, too, or as a dip for raw vegies and rice crackers. It also freezes well.

A GREAT RANGE OF TOFU can be found in Asian food stores.

SOAK BAMBOO SKEWERS in water for a few hours before using, otherwise they tend to burn.

MAKES ABOUT 20

40 g (1/4 cup) sesame seeds

100 g (1/2 cup) raw unhulled buckwheat

150 g (1 1/2 cups) rolled oats

65 g (3/4 cup) quinoa flakes

45 g (1/3 cup) roughly chopped cashews

45 g (1/4 cup) pumpkin seeds (pepitas)

40 g (1/2 cup) shredded coconut

2 tablespoons chia seeds

2 tablespoons sunflower seed kernels

3 teaspoons ground cinnamon

2 teaspoons ground ginger

1 teaspoon ground cumin

1 teaspoon cumin seeds

2 tablespoons melted virgin coconut oil

2 tablespoons tahini

170 g (1/2 cup) rice malt syrup

This recipe is from Incredible Bakes (That Just Happen to be Refined-Sugar Free) *by Caroline Griffiths published by Smith Street Books, RRP $39.99, available in stores nationally. With triple-tested recipes that are completely delicious, natural sweetness is added using whole fruits and, sometimes, other non-fructose sweeteners, including rice malt syrup, dextrose and stevia.*

SUPERFOOD BARS

Super crunchy and packed with protein from seeds and grains, these bars are a tasty energy source after a hard workout or a long walk, or for a relatively healthy snack. It might seem a bit weird to include cumin in a non-savoury recipe, but it gives a slightly unusual and very tasty edge to these bars.

Preheat the oven to 160°C (140°C fan-forced). Grease a 20 cm x 30 cm slice pan and line the base and two long sides with a piece of non-stick baking paper, extending the paper about 4 cm above the sides of the pan to assist with removal of the cooked slice.

Reserving 1 tablespoon of the sesame seeds for sprinkling over the top, combine the remaining sesame seeds and all of the remaining dry ingredients in a large bowl. Add the coconut oil and tahini and mix well until all the ingredients are coated. Drizzle over the syrup and mix until well combined. If you use your hands this job will be easier.

Using the back of a large spoon, press the mixture firmly and evenly into the prepared pan. Sprinkle with the reserved sesame seeds and press them into the surface.

Bake for 25–30 minutes or until the top is firm to touch and lightly browned. Leave the slice in the tin and, while still warm, cut into 20 bars. Place the tin on a wire rack to cool completely.

Store in an airtight container for up to a week.

SCRUMPTIOUS RAW CACAO BALLS

MAKES 12–16

1 cup pitted dates

1 cup almonds

1/3 cup raw cacao powder

1/2 cup natural shredded coconut

1/3 cup organic virgin coconut oil

2 tablespoons chia seeds

shredded coconut, chopped pistachios, flaxseed, or anything else for rolling the balls

I have been making these little treats for a long time and they taste absolutely delicious, are super quick and easy to make and are a great healthy snack to grab on the run. I sometimes even have them for breakfast with my smoothie. They are packed full of energy and superfoods and are a great guilt-free alternative to chocolate if you get hit with 3 o'clock cravings. The recipe can be easily altered to your liking, so don't hesitate to experiment with different ingredients.

Soak dates in warm water for 15 minutes to soften. Drain.

Add nuts, cacao, shredded coconut, coconut oil and chia seeds to blender and mix to a smooth consistency.

Add dates and a teaspoon of filtered water and mix again, making sure the dates are completely blended and there are no chunks.

Let mixture sit for 15 minutes.

Roll mixture into bite-size balls.

Roll balls in coating of your choice and store in a sealed container in the fridge.

The balls will keep for a few days.

Notes:

SHREDDED COCONUT
sometimes has added sugar. Check the label carefully and choose one without added sugar.

HEMP PROTEIN POWDER
can be added – just a small scoop for a further boost.

CHEESY IDEAS

We know a lot of people struggle with the no-dairy component of a vegan diet, but you'll soon discover that plant-based cheeses and butters are lighter options that don't sacrifice flavour or quality and taste like the real thing. Because of our cheese-making background, we understand how vegan cheese products should taste if they are to replace dairy. Whether you're whipping up a snack, taking lunch to work, or going on a picnic, here are some great ideas for incorporating vegan cheeses into your diet.

SMASH SOME AVOCADO with zataar on toasted sourdough spread with cashew feta cheese.

CUT AN AVOCADO IN HALF, remove the stone and fill the hole with vegan feta. The humble avocado never fails to satisfy. Garnish with salt and pepper and fresh parsley or whatever takes your fancy. This simple and quick snack will keep you going for hours.

SPREAD A WRAP with creamy and spreadable vegan cheese, and roll up with fresh salad ingredients.

MAKE A TOASTIE with creamy vegan feta or soft cheese and your favourite fresh ingredients.

MAKE A VEGAN CAPRESE SALAD with creamy vegan cheese, basil and the freshest tastiest tomatoes you can find. It's vegan and lactose free. Our Red Bell Pepper Soft Cheese is perfect for this.

MAKE A CHEESE PLATTER with vegan soft cheese or feta as the hero, alongside your favourite fruits, nuts, vegetables and other tasty dips.

STIR VEGAN FETA through pasta, or heap over steamy baked potatoes.

PUT A LITTLE VEGAN FETA in the bottom of a screw-top jar and fill the jar with carrot and celery sticks – this is a great snack to go, or a lunch on the run.

DAN MAIO

Drummer, The Getaway Plan and Ecca Vandal

The amazing thing about being vegan is that you can actually make a difference and save animals, the planet and yourself just by making a choice three times a day about what you put on your plate. It really is that simple. The past few years have been the best of my life so far. Is it because of veganism? I dunno, but it's made me a much happier and more thoughtful person. I'm not going back.

It's funny how big things can start in a very small way. Gearing up for a holiday to Perth with my family, all I could think about was getting my fishing rods ready. On the last day, Dad and I hooked a bunch of fish. After I'd taken my 'happy fisherman' photo, I got that sick feeling you get when you're a kid and you know you've done something wrong. I held in my hands one of the prettiest fish I'd ever seen. He was scared and oxygen-deprived, and I'd torn almost his entire bottom lip all the way around. I suddenly realised that my fun was at an animal's expense.

That was April 2014, and within weeks I made the choice to be vegan. My brother had planted the seed of change years ago, jumping ship to become vegan. We used to look at him as the crazy one in the family! Now I had found my real place in the food chain too, and it was alongside our animal friends.

I had been fishing for ten years, and it should have been obvious to me from the struggle and panic I had witnessed that fish feel pain, just like all animals do. I've since learnt that fish are actually

Dan with Morgan *(Photo credit: Mike Maio)*

quite intelligent. They can recognise each other, communicate, and grieve the loss of their companions. I replaced fishing with snorkelling and now swimming beside sea life is an experience many times better than fishing ever was. I am also glad to play no further part in the destruction of our oceans.

When I'm on tour, nine times out of ten we're in capital cities and these days there are so many great places to eat, it's super easy. There are little Vs popping up on menus everywhere and damn it makes me happy! It takes five seconds to ask a few questions about what's in the food on a menu, and yeah, you might feel like you're being a pain, but in those few seconds you're saving an animal a heap of real pain.

Music makes me go absolutely crazy! And going crazy behind a drum set takes quite a physical toll. But since changing my diet, I find my body repairs after shows much faster so that sometimes I wake up feeling like I never played a show in the first place.

It's not as if I'm not allowed to eat certain things; it's just that now I know how these products got to my plate, I sure as hell don't want to eat them!

LUNCH & DINNER

small things
salads
mains
comfort food

BLACK BEAN DUMPLINGS, CORN PUREE & SAKE FOAM

MAKES AROUND 45 DUMPLINGS

600 g firm tofu, drained overnight (see note)

4 tablespoons black bean sauce

50 g finely sliced spring onion

salt, to taste

100 g asparagus, finely sliced

vegetable oil, for frying

2 x packs of 24 wonton wrappers

coriander and micro shiso salad, to serve

CORN PUREE

3 shallots, sliced

3 cloves garlic, sliced

vegetable oil, for cooking

1 litre vegetable stock

1 kg frozen corn

salt

SAKE FOAM – see next page

This dish is pure class, a perfect combination of high-end textural contrast and down-home deliciousness. If you really want to knock some socks off, follow up with the cashew parfait and coconut musk dessert on page 171.

FOR THE CORN PUREE, sweat the shallots and garlic with a little oil in a large saucepan until softened. Add the vegetable stock and corn, cover with a lid and simmer for 5 minutes.

Remove from the heat and blend in a food processor until smooth. Season with salt to taste.

FOR THE DUMPLINGS, break up the tofu in a large bowl and fold in the black bean sauce, spring onion and salt to taste.

Sauté the asparagus briefly with oil and a pinch of salt in a hot frying pan. Remove from pan, and place on a plate to cool to room temperature to retain the colour.

Take a wrapper and place a small amount of asparagus in the middle, followed by 1 tablespoon of the tofu mixture. Using a small brush, wipe the corners with a small amount of water. Bring all the corners of the wrapper together, twist and pinch to seal. Repeat with remaining wrappers and filling.

Steam dumplings for 5 minutes.

BLACK BEAN DUMPLINGS, CORN PUREE & SAKE FOAM

SAKE FOAM

230 ml sake

60 ml 1:1 sugar syrup

35 ml yuzu juice

1/2 tablespoon soy lecithin powder

TO MAKE THE SAKE FOAM, combine sake, sugar syrup and yuzu juice and blend with a stick blender while adding the soy lecithin, incorporating air into the mixture to form bubbles.

Serve steamed dumplings with corn puree, add coriander and micro shiso salad, and finish with sake foam.

Notes:

1:1 SUGAR SYRUP is made by bringing equal parts caster sugar and water to the boil. When sugar has dissolved, remove from the heat and cool before use.

YUZU JUICE (from a variety of citrus grown in Japan) can be found at Asian grocery stores.

TO DRAIN TOFU OVERNIGHT, wrap in a clean tea towel and place in a colander. Put the colander over a bowl to catch the liquid that will drain through, and leave in the fridge.

GOLDEN CAULIFLOWER CHIA FRITTERS WITH GREEN TAHINI DIP

MAKES ABOUT 20 FRITTERS

3/4 cup chickpea (besan) flour, plus extra to adjust consistency if needed

2 tablespoons chia seeds

1 tablespoon sweet paprika

1 teaspoon salt (we use sea salt)

1 teaspoon bicarbonate of soda, optional (if you like your fritters fluffy)

1/4 teaspoon ground turmeric

pinch of cayenne pepper

cracked black pepper, to taste

1 small head or 1/2 large cauliflower, coarsely grated

4 spring onions, chopped

1/2 bunch parsley, leaves and stalks chopped (roughly 1 cup)

1 cup rice milk, or other plant milk, plus extra to adjust consistency, if needed

coconut oil, for frying

GREEN TAHINI DIP – see next page

This must be one of the best ways to eat this cancer-fighting cruciferous vegetable. I like to make these delicious little golden things for anyone who allows me into their kitchen! A handy snack to have in the fridge or freezer, they also make sexy finger food. They can even star as a main act for dinner, accompanied by a grand salad. Enjoy the versatility!

FOR THE FRITTERS, mix the dry ingredients in a large bowl. Add the remaining ingredients (except coconut oil) and mix thoroughly. Leave to stand for 30 minutes (this gives the chia seeds, which are acting as an egg replacement, a chance to expand and therefore hold the fritters together).

Check the consistency of the fritter mixture and adjust with extra rice milk or chickpea flour to achieve a consistency that will hold together when fried. (It's a good idea to make and test-fry one fritter before doing all of them.)

Form the fritter mixture into little rounds with wet hands. Heat a large frying pan over medium heat and, working in batches, fry the fritters in coconut oil for about 5 minutes on each side or until golden brown and cauliflower is cooked through in the middle. You can also keep the fritters in a warm oven until ready to serve, which will give them another chance to cook through.

Serve with green tahini dip.

GOLDEN CAULIFLOWER CHIA FRITTERS WITH GREEN TAHINI DIP

GREEN TAHINI DIP

1/2 cup hulled tahini

1/4 cup lemon juice

2 tablespoons apple cider vinegar

1–2 cloves garlic, chopped

1/2 teaspoon salt

1 cup parsley leaves, chopped
(coriander and mint work well too)

FOR THE DIP, place all the ingredients in a blender and blend with ½–1 cup of water to achieve the desired consistency. (Dip will keep for 4–5 days in an airtight container in the fridge, and freezes well too.)

Notes:

A REALLY GOOD TAHINI SAUCE recipe is essential for every good vegan chef, and this dip is it. Serve it as a dip with vegie sticks, crackers, chips, salad – the possibilities are endless. Whenever you're using tahini remember to stir it in the jar very well with a clean spoon first. This will ensure that the thick sediment at the bottom is blended with the oily part on top.

LEFTOVER COOKED GRAINS such as millet or quinoa can be used in this recipe – simply add 1 cup to the fritter mixture.

SERVES 2-4

1-2 tablespoons of rice bran oil

1 large onion, finely diced

1 teaspoon minced garlic

500 ml water

250 ml Bonsoy soy milk

1 teaspoon of salt

plenty of freshly ground pepper, to taste

1-2 teaspoons liquid smoke, depending on your liking for strong flavours

6 teaspoons Massel vegetable stock powder

2 large brown potatoes, peeled and cut into small cubes (approx. 4 cups)

4 medium zucchini, grated (approx. 4 cups)

2 cups corn kernels

Notes:

LIQUID SMOKE is available at well-stocked delis and USAFoods, which is also online.

GARNISH with some thin slices of red capsicum or long red chilli for extra taste and a splash of colour if you wish.

ZUCCHINI (AND NO BACON) CHOWDER

This soup proves you can have bold flavour without bacon. It's best served straight away, with your favourite crusty bread.

Heat the oil in a large pot on a low to medium heat. Sauté the onion gently until browned. Add the garlic and cook for another minute or so.

Add the water, Bonsoy, salt, pepper, liquid smoke, stock powder and potato and bring to the boil. Once the water has boiled, turn the heat down to a very gentle simmer. (You don't want to reduce the stock too much so avoid a furious boil at this stage.) Simmer until the potato cubes are cooked about halfway through.

Add half the zucchini and cover your pot. The soup will look like it needs way more water but don't be tempted to add more liquid at this point because zucchini contains a ton of water. Just continue cooking for a few minutes until the potato is on the cusp of being ready. Turn the heat off.

Using a ladle, scoop out half the soup into another container. Try to ladle a lot of the liquid into the container as well as potato and zucchini. Blend the mixture in the container until it is smooth. Add the blended soup back into the pot with the unblended soup and gently stir to combine. Try not to break up the lovely potato chunks as you do this. Throw the rest of the zucchini and corn in, bring the soup to the boil and serve immediately.

SOUPA RISI

SERVES 4–6

olive oil, for frying

2 medium onions, finely chopped

2 small carrots, finely chopped

2 stalks celery, finely chopped

2.5 litres vegetable stock, or 3 chicken-style stock cubes (Massel) dissolved in 2.5 litres water

1 cup basmati rice

125 g silken tofu

juice of 1 lemon

1/4 cup olive oil

salt (we use Himalayan or Celtic sea salt)

hot crusty bread, to serve

olive and cucumber salad, to serve (optional)

Based on a traditional Greek Cypriot recipe, this tofu and lemon rice soup is a firm favourite at Dolly's. I always make a huge pot full to the top, and it always disappears within a few hours.

Heat a little olive oil in a large saucepan and fry the onion, carrot and celery for 5 minutes, or until softened.

Add the stock and bring to the boil, then add the rice. Boil until the rice is cooked and the vegies are very tender.

Blend the tofu with the lemon juice in a blender or with a stick blender until smooth. Pour three-quarters of the tofu mixture into the saucepan, stirring constantly. Try the soup and add the remaining tofu and lemon to taste.

Season with salt to taste and serve with hot crusty bread and an olive and cucumber salad, if desired.

PUMPKIN COCONUT SOUP

MAKES ABOUT 20 CUPS

3 onions

4 cloves garlic

egg-size piece of ginger, peeled

1/3 cup olive oil

4 tablespoons of powdered vegie stock

3 litres water

1 large pumpkin, 2.5–3 kg

250 ml coconut cream

extra coconut cream, to serve (optional)

This soup is silky smooth, creamy and delicious. It's super easy, so make a big batch and freeze some for later so you have a quick lunch on hand. It's nutritious, and a family favourite every time. We use butternut pumpkin and Jap pumpkin works well too.

Peel and dice the onions.

Heat the oil in a frying pan then fry onions until soft.

Finely chop the garlic and grate the ginger.

Add garlic and ginger to onions and fry until golden brown. Transfer to a large pot.

Add the water and vegie stock and bring to the boil.

Peel and roughly chop the pumpkin into small pieces. Add to the boiling water and cook until very soft.

Zhooozsh with a stick blender until smooth and lump-free. Do this in batches.

Add coconut cream and mix well.

Serve with a dollop of coconut cream on top and cracked black pepper. It's delicious with crunchy herb and garlic bread.

'HEARTS THAT
BEAT TO THE TUNE
OF KINDNESS CAN
CHANGE THE RHYTHM
OF THE WORLD.'

CJ Peterson

FENNEL, RED CABBAGE & CARROT SLAW

SERVES 4 AS A SIDE

1/4 small red cabbage, finely shredded with a mandolin

1 small bulb fennel, finely shredded with a mandolin

2 medium carrots, cut into ribbons with a spiralizer

APPLE CIDER VINAIGRETTE

1/3 cup extra virgin olive oil

1/4 cup raw apple cider vinegar

2 tablespoons lemon juice

1 tablespoon Dijon mustard

1–2 tablespoons maple syrup, to taste

salt and pepper, to taste

This vibrant coleslaw is the salad component in The Kindness Burger on page 142 – but it is also much, much more. Not only is it a delicious side with any kind of grilled tofu or mushroom you can think of, but also a great jumping-off point for all your coleslaw cookery. Try using different types of crunchy vegetables, adding toasted nuts or seeds, or even beans.

For the vinaigrette, combine all the ingredients in a clean screw-top jar and shake until smooth. Taste and adjust the sweetness and seasoning as required.

Place all the vegetables in a large bowl and toss with the dressing until well combined.

Notes:

NO MANDOLIN OR SPIRALIZER? Shred the cabbage as finely as you can with a knife. Cut the fennel and carrot into thin slices with a vegetable peeler, and then into thin strips with a knife.

WARM KALE SALAD WITH TAHINI & MISO PASTE

SERVES 1–2

sesame oil, for frying

1 teaspoon finely chopped garlic

3 cups roughly chopped kale (I like curly kale, or a mix of different types)

handful of thinly sliced red cabbage

handful of thinly sliced white cabbage

handful of grated carrot

3 tablespoons chopped walnuts, plus extra to serve

black and white sesame seeds, to serve

lemon wedges, to serve

TAHINI & MISO PASTE – see next page

It's the little touches that make this warm salad full of hearty umami flavours so special. The tahini and miso paste takes only moments to prepare and then just keeps on giving, not only in depth of flavour but also in future salads. As for the tamari pepitas, be warned, some may be lost to snacking – you might want to make double to be on the safe side!

FOR THE TAHINI AND MISO PASTE, place all ingredients in a bowl, mix to combine thoroughly and store in a sealed jar in the fridge (it will keep for months).

FOR THE TAMARI PEPITAS, heat a non-stick frying pan over medium heat. Add the pepitas and roast, shaking the pan, until they start to pop. Add a little tamari and shake the pan to coat the seeds. Turn the heat right down and keep shaking the pan until pepitas have a dry, roasted, golden coating. Allow to cool on a plate lined with baking paper and store in a sealed container.

TAHINI & MISO PASTE

1 cup tahini (use the best quality you can find)

3 heaped tablespoons vegan miso paste

2 tablespoons agave or rice malt syrup

2 1/2 tablespoons tamari, or to taste

pinch of salt

TAMARI PEPITAS

1/2 cup pepitas

2 tablespoons tamari

TO MAKE THE SALAD, heat a large frying pan on high heat. Add a big slug of sesame oil and the garlic. Cook briefly, then add kale, red and white cabbage and grated carrot. Stir to lightly coat the vegetables and fry until kale is softened but still a vibrant green colour.

Stir in the walnuts, then add 2 heaped tablespoons of tahini and miso paste, and about 1/4 cup water. (You could also add the cabbage and carrot now if you prefer your vegies crispier.)

Using a wooden spoon, stir to break up the paste, making sure the vegies are evenly coated. Remove from the heat.

Serve topped with extra chopped walnuts, mixed sesame seeds and the tamari pepitas, with lemon wedges on the side.

Notes:

VEGAN MISO PASTE does not contain bonito (dried tuna shavings used in dashi stocks and flavourings) and is available from some supermarkets, health food stores and Asian grocers. Check the label carefully.

LEBANESE PEARL COUSCOUS, PUMPKIN, SAFFRON & FIGS

SERVES 6–8

500 g Lebanese pearl couscous

1 kg butternut pumpkin, peeled and cut into roughly 2.5 cm cubes

olive oil, for cooking

salt

1 brown onion, diced

1 litre saffron stock

2 zucchini, diced

200 g dried figs, rehydrated in warm water and halved

lemon juice, to taste

Aleppo pepper, to taste

1 bunch coriander, leaves picked and chopped, to serve

100 g blanched almonds, roasted and chopped, to serve

SAFFRON STOCK – see next page

Here are three of my favourite things: pearl couscous, pumpkin and saffron, combined to create a lovely satisfying meal full of big, bright flavours. The Aleppo pepper gives it an extra kick at the end, and is worth tracking down at a Turkish grocery store, but roasted chilli flakes will work too.

Preheat the oven to 170°C.

Cook the couscous in salted water for 8 minutes and set aside to cool.

Season the pumpkin with olive oil and salt and roast in the oven until golden and cubes are starting to soften but still hold their shape, around 25 minutes. Remove half of the pumpkin and set aside. Allow the other half to keep roasting until caramelised and completely soft, around 15 minutes. Put the soft pumpkin in a bowl and smash with a whisk until pureed.

In a hot saucepan, add a dash of oil and sauté the onion until softened. Add the pumpkin 'puree' and allow to cook out until it starts to catch on the bottom of the pan, then stir in the saffron stock, Lebanese couscous, zucchini and the firm pumpkin cubes. It should have a nice thick consistency.

When the pumpkin and zucchini are just softened, add the dried figs, and season with lemon juice, Aleppo pepper and salt to taste.

Before serving, sprinkle the fresh coriander and roasted almonds on top.

LEBANESE PEARL COUSCOUS, PUMPKIN, SAFFRON & FIGS

SAFFRON STOCK

2 carrots, diced

1 head celery, diced

3 onions, diced

5 tomatoes, quartered

6 cloves garlic

olive oil, for sautéing

pinch of saffron

10 sprigs thyme

4 bay leaves

FOR THE SAFFRON STOCK, sauté all the vegetables with a little olive oil in a hot saucepan until golden. Add the saffron, thyme and bay leaves and cover with 5 litres of water. Bring to the boil and allow to simmer for 2 hours.

Strain through a muslin-lined sieve and set aside until required. The stock freezes well so have some on hand for the next time you make this dish.

Notes:

WHEN FIGS ARE IN SEASON, try leaving out the dried figs and serving with fresh figs.

ALEPPO PEPPER gives an extra kick at the end, and is worth tracking down at a Turkish grocery store, but roasted chilli flakes will work too.

KALE SUPERSALAD WITH GOJI & GINGER DRESSING

SERVES 4

1 medium beetroot, cut into matchsticks

2 tablespoons apple cider vinegar with the mother

1 large bunch kale, stems removed, leaves torn into bite-size pieces

extra virgin olive oil

good quality salt (we use sea salt or rock salt)

2 medium carrots, cut into matchsticks

handful of flat-leaf parsley leaves

handful of shredded red cabbage

1/4 cup goji berries

2 tablespoons chia seeds

1/2 cup pepitas (preferably activated and organic)

organic seed crackers or cooked quinoa, to serve, optional

GOJI & GINGER DRESSING – see next page

This nutritionally charged salad is a true superhero of a meal, not only loaded with plant protein, but dense with vitamins, minerals and antioxidants to boost the immune system. The creamy, tangy dressing is also a nutritional powerhouse and, depending on how 'saucy' you like your salad, you'll probably have some left over. It will keep in a clean glass jar in the fridge for at least a couple of weeks and you'll find plenty of other ways to use it ... on raw and cooked vegies, or even just to dip your carrot sticks in for an awesome snack!

Toss the beetroot with the apple cider vinegar in a bowl and leave to stand for a couple of hours to soften. (I sometimes leave it to marinate overnight or even for a couple of days in a container in the fridge.)

FOR THE DRESSING, place the goji berries in a bowl with the apple cider vinegar, lemon juice and 1 tablespoon water and leave to stand for about 15 minutes or so to soften (this is important to achieve a smooth result). Place the remaining ingredients in a blender (or food processor), add the goji berries and soaking liquid, and blend until smooth. If too thick, add a dash of water. Taste and adjust the seasoning with extra coconut syrup, cayenne pepper or salt if required.

KALE SUPERSALAD WITH GOJI & GINGER DRESSING

GOJI & GINGER DRESSING

50 g goji berries

40 ml apple cider vinegar with the mother

40 ml lemon juice

1/2 tablespoon coconut syrup

1–2 teaspoons grated fresh ginger, or to taste

1 teaspoon ground ginger

100 ml extra virgin olive oil

2 tablespoons tahini

1/2 teaspoon ground cumin

pinch of cayenne pepper

1/2 teaspoon salt, or to taste

Place the kale in a large bowl, drizzle with a little olive oil, sprinkle with salt and give it a good, firm massage with clean hands to break down the fibres and soften.

Add the carrot to the bowl with the kale, along with the marinated beetroot (add the cider vinegar used to marinate the beetroot if you like, or set aside for another use), the parsley, cabbage, goji berries, and a drizzle of dressing. Sprinkle the chia seeds over the top (they will form lumps if you just dump them in so make sure you sprinkle!) and toss thoroughly.

If you can bear to wait, refrigerate the salad for an hour or two to marinate and allow the goji berries and chia to soften and soak up all the lovely flavours.

When you are ready to eat, check whether you need to add a sprinkle more salt and toss through half the pepitas. Add an extra splash of dressing, sprinkle the remaining pepitas on top and serve with seed crackers or cooked quinoa, if desired.

Notes:

BEETROOT AND CARROT should be sliced with a mandolin or V slicer if you have one.

BRAGG APPLE CIDER VINEGAR (with the 'mother') is an unrefined vinegar that still contains some of the proteins, enzymes and friendly bacteria used in the fermentation process. It can be found in health food stores. Substitute regular apple cider vinegar.

COCONUT SYRUP is a natural sweetener derived from coconut blossom and can be found in health food stores and some supermarkets.

SERVES 4

400 g block firm tofu, fried if available, cut into 2 cm cubes

2 tablespoons rice bran oil (or sunflower oil)

200 g rice vermicelli noodles, cooked, cooled in iced water and drained thoroughly

1 red capsicum, deseeded, quartered and finely sliced

2 Lebanese cucumbers, cored and julienned using a mandolin

1 medium red onion, finely sliced

2 long red chillies, halved, seeded and thinly sliced lengthways, optional

1 bunch mint, leaves picked, large leaves torn

1 bunch coriander, leaves picked

1 bunch Thai basil, leaves picked, large leaves torn

4 kaffir lime leaves, centre veins removed, finely shredded

55 g roasted peanuts, coarsely chopped

DRESSING – see next page

FRAGRANT THAI TOFU SALAD

This is what street food is all about – easy, fresh, vibrant and perfect for any occasion. Think dinner on a hot summer's night, a mid-week packed lunch pick-me-up, or a lively addition to a shared table. This salad has got you sorted!

MAKE THE DRESSING – see next page.

FOR THE TOFU, place the cubed tofu in a glass or ceramic dish. Drizzle with half the dressing. Cover with plastic wrap and place in the fridge, turning occasionally, for 2 hours to develop the flavours.

Preheat a barbecue grill or chargrill pan on high. Brush grill or pan with the oil and cook the tofu for 5–6 minutes, turning occasionally to make sure the cubes are evenly browned. Brush with the marinade as you turn.

Place the noodles, capsicum, cucumber, onion, chilli, mint, coriander, Thai basil, lime leaves and peanuts in a large bowl. Add the grilled tofu, drizzle with the remaining dressing and gently toss to combine.

Divide salad among bowls, garnish with coriander and serve immediately.

FRAGRANT THAI TOFU SALAD

DRESSING

2 teaspoons finely grated ginger

1 clove garlic, crushed

1/2 stalk lemongrass, inner white part only, crushed in mortar and pestle and chopped finely

2 tablespoons lime juice

1 tablespoon vegan fish sauce (or light soy sauce)

2 teaspoons sesame oil

1 teaspoon tamari

1 tablespoon coconut sugar (if unable to source, replace with raw or brown sugar)

FOR THE DRESSING, whisk together the ginger, garlic, lemongrass, lime juice, vegan fish sauce, sesame oil, tamari and sugar in a jug.

Notes:

VEGAN FISH SAUCE is amazing. We use Vincent Vegetarian Food brand.

NO MANDOLIN? Just cut the vegies into 2 mm matchsticks.

SERVES 3–4

1/2 x 270 g packet soba noodles

20 ml toasted sesame oil

1/3 x 340 g packet kelp noodles, soaked

75 g baby spinach leaves, blanched and refreshed

20 g arame, soaked in warm water for 15 minutes

15 g goji berries, soaked in warm water for 15 minutes

1 bunch broccolini, blanched, refreshed and cut into 3 cm pieces

pickled ginger, to serve

shredded nori, to serve

toasted black and white sesame seeds, to serve

DRESSING

100 g vegan miso paste

100 ml rice vinegar

1 teaspoon tamari

30 ml toasted sesame oil

60 ml grapeseed oil

WASABI CASHEWS

100 g cashews

15 g caster sugar

1 teaspoon wasabi paste

SOBA & KELP NOODLE SALAD WITH GOJI, ARAME & SPINACH

Give your clean green eating a boost with three sea veg and bright goji and wasabi flavours that pop against a solid umami background. So good.

FOR THE WASABI CASHEWS, preheat the oven to 160°C. Spread the cashews on a baking tray and roast until just golden. Remove from the oven and turn the heat down to 100°C.

Combine the sugar and 15 ml water in a small saucepan and bring to the boil. Remove from heat and mix in the wasabi paste, then add the cashews and stir to coat evenly.

Spread the nuts on a baking tray lined with baking paper, spacing them out so they are mostly separate. Roast for 1½–2 hours, until wasabi coating is set and glossy. Turn off the heat and allow to cool in the oven for around 4 hours. Store in a sealed container in the fridge until needed.

FOR THE DRESSING, combine the miso, rice vinegar and tamari in a mixing bowl. Add the sesame and grapeseed oils in a slow stream while continually whisking. Set aside.

Bring a big saucepan of salted water to the boil. Turn down to a simmer, add the soba noodles and cook for 2 minutes while stirring gently. Drain the noodles, cool in an ice-water bath, drain again and then coat in toasted sesame oil.

Combine soba and kelp noodles, spinach, arame, goji berries and broccolini and toss with the dressing. Garnish with pickled ginger, nori and sesame seeds.

RAW PAD THAI SALAD

SERVES 4–6

3 medium zucchini, cut into matchsticks or julienned

1/4 red cabbage, shredded

4 large carrots, cut into matchsticks or julienned

3 large red capsicums, thinly sliced

50 g snow peas, trimmed and thinly sliced

2 handfuls of mint leaves

large handful of peanuts, to serve

DRESSING

200 g peanut butter

1/4 cup tamari

30 ml sesame oil

30 ml lime juice

1 1/2 tablespoons rice malt syrup

2.5 cm piece ginger

1 clove garlic

pinch of cayenne pepper

This beautiful rainbow salad is a crisp, nutrient-rich take on the classic Thai noodle dish. It's full of enzymes, vitamins and minerals, and tastes as amazing as it looks. Use the freshest vegetables for this salad, as you will be able to taste each and every one. Serve with love and gratitude and enjoy!

Place all the salad ingredients except the peanuts in a large bowl and toss to combine.

FOR THE DRESSING, blend all the ingredients and 30 ml water in a blender for 2 minutes until smooth.

Sprinkle the peanuts over the top of the salad and serve with the dressing on the side.

NUTRITION BOMB

SERVES 4

500 g Jap pumpkin, cut into 5 cm cubes

1 medium sweet potato, cut into 5 cm cubes

2 handfuls of broccoli florets

4 handfuls of baby spinach leaves

2 handfuls of alfalfa sprouts

4 handfuls of kale leaves

2 handfuls of cherry tomatoes, sliced or halved

2 avocados, sliced

1 tablespoon sesame seeds (mixture of black and white), to serve

lemon wedges, to serve

SAUERKRAUT

1/2 white cabbage, shredded

1/2 red cabbage, shredded

2 pinches of salt

HUMMUS – see next page

This is our signature dish and the first on our menu. It is the perfect combination of good fats, fermented vegetables and complex carbohydrates. The probiotics in the sauerkraut leave your gut feeling happy, while the tryptophan in the sweet potato converts to serotonin, for a happy mood. Prepare the sauerkraut and hummus in advance to allow for fermenting and soaking time.

FOR THE SAUERKRAUT, mix the shredded cabbage with the salt in a large bowl. Allow to ferment for a few days until soft, ensuring you mix it every day.

TO MAKE THE HUMMUS, bring 800 ml water to the boil in a large saucepan. Add the chickpeas and cook until soft. Drain the chickpeas, retaining the cooking water.

Place the chickpeas in a food processor and blend, slowly adding small amounts of cooking water until the desired consistency is achieved. Add the tahini, lemon juice and salt to taste, and blend until well combined.

Preheat the oven to 200°C.

Line two baking trays with baking paper. Place the pumpkin pieces on one tray and the sweet potato on the other, as they will take different times to cook. Roast until tender, checking after 5–10 minutes.

NUTRITION BOMB

HUMMUS

200 g chickpeas, soaked for 8 hours or overnight

20 g raw tahini

lemon juice, to taste

2 pinches of salt, or to taste

Meanwhile, steam the broccoli, or boil for 2–3 minutes then blanch in iced water to retain the colour.

To assemble, place a handful of spinach leaves in each bowl and place a dollop of hummus in the centre. Arrange sauerkraut, broccoli, alfalfa, kale, pumpkin, sweet potato and cherry tomatoes around the hummus and top with sliced avocado, sesame seeds and a wedge of lemon.

Notes:

USE CANNED CHICKPEAS if you forget to soak the chickpeas (it happens!). Simply substitute 2 x 400 g cans and process as above, adding water as necessary.

WITH THE SAUERKRAUT, you will have more than you need for this recipe. It will keep well in a jar in the fridge and is great as a side or sandwich ingredient.

RAINBOW TART WITH CHUNKY PESTO

SERVES 10

2 1/2 cups chickpea (besan) flour

1/2 cup olive oil, plus extra for baking

1 kg pumpkin, peeled and roughly diced

salt and pepper

Italian dried herbs, to taste

6 medium beetroot, unpeeled

1 bunch spinach, washed and roughly chopped

liquid smoke, optional

PESTO

1 bunch basil

large handful of rocket

1–1 1/2 cups oil of your choice

juice of 1 lemon

crushed garlic, to taste

salt and pepper

4 cups almonds

Both this colourful tart and the fresh pesto are complete originals, and favourites at Pollen 185. They are foolproof, super delicious and very filling. I recommend you use the recipe as a guide and go from there. Love garlic? Add more garlic! Love mint? Put some in the pesto! Leftover tart is delicious cold the next day.

Preheat the oven to 180°C.

TO MAKE THE TART BASE, combine the chickpea flour and olive oil in a bowl and add warm water slowly until the mixture has a pastry consistency. Press into a 25 cm loose-bottom flan tin with your knuckles – it doesn't have to be perfect but it does need to cover the whole base. If you don't have enough dough, just whip up a tiny bit more and press into the holes.

Prick the base with a fork about 9 times and bake for 8–10 minutes until slightly springy to the touch, but not soft. Remove from the oven but don't turn the oven off. Allow base to cool and refrigerate until ready to use. (You can make the base the night before if you like.)

Place the pumpkin in a big baking dish and toss with a healthy amount of olive oil, salt, pepper and herbs. Bake in the oven until cooked through, 15–20 minutes (I like to have some of the pieces a little on the caramelised side).

Meanwhile, boil the beetroot in a large saucepan of water until just soft. Drain and set aside.

RAINBOW TART WITH CHUNKY PESTO

Cook the spinach in a saucepan with a few centimetres of water until just wilted through. Cool a little and then blend until smooth.

Discard the skins and tails from the beetroot and chop roughly. Blend using whatever kitchen appliance you have until silky smooth.

When the pumpkin is cooked and has cooled enough to handle, add a little liquid smoke, if using, and squish with your hands to break it down, retaining some texture.

TO ASSEMBLE, cover the whole tart base with the spinach puree, then the pumpkin mixture, taking care to keep the layers separate (this is much easier to do with your hands, when the pumpkin is warm). I like to let a little bit of spinach show through on the edges for a rustic touch.

Spread the beetroot mixture on top from the middle out, leaving some pumpkin and spinach showing.

Refrigerate the tart for at least a few hours so the layers don't blend when sliced.

Shortly before serving, preheat the oven to 180°C and transfer the tart to a baking tray lined with baking paper. Place in the oven until just warmed through – about 5 minutes.

TO MAKE THE PESTO, place the basil, rocket, 1 cup oil, lemon juice, garlic, and salt and pepper to taste in the bowl of a food processor and process until smooth.

Add the almonds and extra oil if you think it needs it, and pulse until only just chopped up. Check the salt, garlic, lemon and oil levels, stirring in any additions by hand.

Serve slices of tart with a generous dollop of pesto.

Notes:

PESTO will keep for a week in a jar in the fridge, with just a little extra oil on top.

LIQUID SMOKE is available from gourmet and specialty grocery stores.

GRATE THE COOKED BEETROOT to add texture.

BROCCOLI & ASPARAGUS WITH WILD RICE, TRUFFLED MISO AIOLI & WALNUT

SERVES 4

1 cup wild rice

sea salt flakes

freshly cracked pepper

2 heads broccoli, florets trimmed from stems (to yield about 300 g)

2 bunches asparagus, bottom third trimmed and discarded

1/2 cup lightly toasted walnuts, finely grated (we use a Microplane grater)

1 punnet micro shiso, optional

TRUFFLED MISO AIOLI

2 tablespoons water drained from canned chickpeas

1 tablespoon shiro (white) miso paste

1 1/2 teaspoons sherry vinegar (or any wine vinegar)

3/4 cup grapeseed or sunflower oil

1 teaspoon truffle oil

LEMON OIL – see next page

Let us count the ways we love this vegan, gluten-free and super tasty dish: it gets a big tick for health, for looks, for kindness, for originality, for being deeelish — but enough counting. More cooking and eating!

FOR THE LEMON OIL, combine the ingredients in a clean bowl or jar, cover and leave on the kitchen bench overnight. Pass the oil through a fine strainer and reserve.

FOR THE TRUFFLED MISO AIOLI, mix the chickpea water, miso and sherry vinegar using a whisk, stick blender or food processor. Add about a quarter of the oil, drop by drop, mixing until emulsified (starting the emulsification is the most difficult part, so be patient). Add the remaining oil in a stream, mixing continuously. Any leftover aioli can be kept in the fridge in an airtight container for a week.

Bring 6 cups of salted water to the boil in a medium saucepan. Add the wild rice and simmer until the grains are tender and have just puffed open, about 40 minutes. Drain the rice and toss in a little lemon oil, sea salt and pepper.

Meanwhile, cut any large broccoli florets in half and cut the asparagus stems in half crossways on a bias. Bring a large saucepan of salted water to a simmer, add the broccoli and cook for 1 minute, then add the asparagus and cook for a further 2 minutes. Drain the broccoli and asparagus well, shaking off any excess water. Toss in a little lemon oil, sea salt and pepper.

BROCCOLI & ASPARAGUS WITH WILD RICE, TRUFFLED MISO AIOLI & WALNUT

LEMON OIL

1 cup good quality extra virgin olive oil

zest of 1 lemon

freshly cracked pepper

Divide the wild rice among four shallow bowls, spreading it out to form a bed for the vegetables. Place the broccoli florets atop the rice and then stand the asparagus spears upright by leaning them on the florets. Spoon four randomly spaced mounds of grated walnut into each bowl. With the aioli, use a squeeze bottle or piping bag with a small tip to create several relatively evenly spaced domes in each bowl. Garnish with micro shiso, if using.

WHOLE BAKED SWEET POTATO WITH MEXICAN SPICED BEANS

SERVES 4

4 small sweet potatoes of equal size

coconut yoghurt, corn chips, coriander leaves, lime wedges, sliced chilli, to serve

APPLE BAKED BEANS

3 x 400 g can black eye beans

1 brown onion, peeled and sliced thinly

1 red capsicum, sliced thinly

1 tablespoon garlic, minced

1 tablespoon chipotle in adobo sauce

125 ml orange juice

1 tablespoon smoked paprika

1 x 800 g can chunky crushed tomatoes

2 tablespoons apple cider vinegar

2 tablespoons brown sugar

80 ml tamari

1 sprig rosemary

2 red apples, chopped into 1 cm cubes

PICO DE GALLO – see next page

This winter heartwarmer has everything you could want to feel satisfied on a chilly evening. Spicy apple baked beans, creamy coconut yoghurt, avocado pico de gallo (salsa), and crunchy corn chips to scoop up everything that lands on the plate.

Preheat the oven to 180°C.

FOR THE SWEET POTATOES, scrub clean with water and pat dry. Toss in some olive or coconut oil, season with salt and pepper and place them on a tray to bake, whole. They will take approximately an hour to get caramelly and soft.

FOR THE BEANS, sauté the onions and capsicum in olive oil until soft, about 8 minutes. Add the garlic and chipotle and cook for a further minute. Add the orange juice and allow to reduce for a few minutes.

Add all remaining ingredients except the apple and simmer gently for about 20 minutes. Add the chopped apple and cook for a further 15 minutes. The beans should be quite thick. Remove the rosemary and season with salt and pepper, to taste.

MAKE THE PICO DE GALLO while the beans are cooking. Cut the corn off the cob and sauté the kernels in some olive or coconut oil in a very hot pan until just softening. Set aside to cool.

WHOLE BAKED SWEET POTATO WITH MEXICAN SPICED BEANS

PICO DE GALLO

olive or coconut oil, for cooking

1 corn cob

1 red capsicum

1 small Lebanese cucumber

1 lime, juiced

1 ripe avocado

Chop the capsicum and cucumber approximately the same size as the corn kernels, taking care to remove the seeds. Toss in a bowl with the lime juice and season with salt and pepper.

Roughly mash the avocado.

TO ASSEMBLE, slice the sweet potatoes in half lengthways, about three-quarters through, open up and place each one on a plate. Pile on the baked beans, top with avocado and a dollop of coconut yoghurt. Stick the corn chips into the yoghurt, and scatter the pico de gallo around the plate. Serve with lime wedges, coriander leaves and fresh chilli, to taste.

Notes:

THE BEAN MIXTURE will easily serve 6, so you might have leftovers. It keeps well for a few days in a sealed container in the fridge.

EGGPLANT CAPONATA

SERVES 4

vegetable oil, for frying

2 large eggplants (about 1 kg), cut into 2 cm cubes

sea salt

3 stalks celery, cut into 1 cm pieces

15 green olives, stoned and halved

50 ml extra virgin olive oil

1 large brown onion, sliced

50 g capers in vinegar

150 g ripe tomatoes, diced

2 tablespoons white vinegar

1 tablespoon white sugar

crusty bread, to serve

This traditional Sicilian dish is vegan, dairy free, gluten free, halal, kosher and delicious, perfect for antipasto or a side dish. Use the best quality produce you can find and prepare it the day before serving to develop the flavours. It can be stored in the fridge for 3–4 days.

Heat a wide, deep pan one-third full of vegetable oil until it reaches 180°C. Fry the eggplant in batches until golden and soft, being careful not to overcrowd the pan and allowing the oil to come back up to temperature between batches. Drain and place on a large platter, then sprinkle with salt.

Bring a saucepan of cold, lightly salted water to boil, add the celery and boil for about 5 minutes. Add the olives and boil for another 2 minutes, then drain and set aside.

Heat the olive oil in a large, wide pan over low–medium heat and fry the onion until it starts to become soft and golden, then add the celery, olives and capers and cook for another 4 minutes, stirring from time to time. Add the tomatoes and cook for another couple of minutes, then add the eggplant and mix gently. Season with salt, then turn the heat right down and simmer gently for 2 minutes. Take the pan off the heat and allow the caponata to cool to room temperature.

In a small saucepan, warm up the vinegar and sugar, stirring until the sugar dissolves. Add the sweet and sour syrup to the caponata and mix gently to combine. Adjust the seasoning to taste and refrigerate overnight.

PAN-FRIED POLENTA WITH OYSTER MUSHROOMS

SERVES 4

olive oil, for frying

400 g pink oyster mushrooms

flat-leaf parsley, chopped, to serve

RAGOUT

60 g brown onion, finely diced

1/2 tablespoon garlic, chopped very finely

4 sprigs thyme

olive oil, for sautéing

400 ml white wine

400 ml vegetable stock

40 g maize cornflour

POLENTA – see next page

VEGETABLE STOCK – see next page

Bring a bit of high fashion to your plant-based kitchen with this stylish homage to a Northern Italian classic. Pink oyster mushrooms are undoubtedly the glamour ingredient here, but if they are unavailable don't despair – regular oyster mushrooms will taste just as good! You will need to start preparing the polenta the night before.

FOR THE STOCK, bring the water to the boil and add the chopped vegetables. Simmer until the liquid has reduced down to 1 litre and then strain.

FOR THE POLENTA, sauté the onion and garlic with olive oil in a medium saucepan until soft and translucent. Add the soy milk, stock, bay leaf and thyme and slowly bring to the boil. Remove the thyme and bay leaf.

Slowly add the polenta, whisking continuously until smooth. Continue cooking until polenta is thick and grains are cooked. Remove from the heat, cover with a lid and leave to rest for approximately 20 minutes.

Mix in the chopped herbs, then roll into a sausage shape and wrap in plastic wrap. Refrigerate for 24 hours.

POLENTA

25 g brown onion, finely diced

1/4 tablespoon garlic, very finely chopped

olive oil, for sautéing

250 ml soy milk

250 ml vegetable stock

1 bay leaf

1 sprig thyme

125 g polenta

50 g flat-leaf parsley, chopped

10 g chives, chopped

VEGETABLE STOCK

4 litres filtered water

150 g carrot, chopped

90 g celeriac, chopped

250 g leek, chopped

150 g onions, quartered

2 bay leaves

6 black peppercorns

1 sprig thyme

FOR THE RAGOUT, sauté the onion, garlic and thyme with a little olive oil in a medium saucepan. Add the white wine and vegetable stock and cook until liquid has reduced by half. Blend the cornflour with 1/2 cup water until smooth, and add to onion mixture, stirring to thicken. Remove the sprig of thyme and keep warm while you fry the polenta and oyster mushrooms.

Cut the polenta into 1.5 cm thick rounds. Heat a large frying pan over medium–high heat and fry polenta pieces in olive oil until browned and crispy on both sides.

In a separate frying pan, fry the oyster mushrooms briefly over high heat with a little olive oil.

To serve, top pan-fried polenta pieces with oyster mushrooms and ragout, and garnish with flat-leaf parsley.

Notes:

OUR OYSTER MUSHROOMS are sourced from Life Cykel, a very cool start-up turning coffee waste into mushrooms. Check out their good work at lifecykel.com.au

SERVES 6

1 large onion, roughly chopped

1 large carrot, roughly chopped

1/2 red capsicum, roughly chopped

small handful of green beans, roughly chopped

1 stalk celery, roughly chopped

1 clove garlic, finely chopped

1 1/2 tablespoons olive oil

1 cup cooked chickpeas

1/2 tablespoon ground turmeric

1 teaspoon garam masala

3 teaspoons ground cumin or cumin seeds

1 tablespoon curry powder, or more according to taste

1/2 teaspoon ground cardamom, or 3 pods, bruised

1/2 tablespoon ground ginger

1/2 large sweet potato, roughly chopped

1 x 400 g can diced or crushed tomatoes

1/2–1 teaspoon rapadura sugar

small splash of Bragg All Purpose Seasoning, optional

pinch of salt (we use Celtic sea salt)

1 1/2 tablespoons tomato paste

cooked basmati rice or quinoa, to serve

salad, to serve

CHICKPEA & VEGIE CURRY

Vegan, vegetarian or omnivore, a good curry is something we can all agree on. This spicy, satisfying chickpea number is a sure-fire crowd pleaser and a delicious healthy meal to boot. If you are not catering for the masses, do yourself a favour and stock up the freezer!

Place the onion, carrot, capsicum, beans, celery and garlic in a large, wide heavy-based saucepan with the olive oil. Fry for several minutes over medium–high heat.

Add the cooked chickpeas, cover and cook for approximately 10 minutes until the beans and carrot are becoming soft, then add all of the spices and the sweet potato.

Add the tomatoes, sugar, seasoning if using, and salt. Stir in 1½ –2 cups water.

Cook until sweet potato is soft and all other vegetables are soft, approximately 15 minutes.

A few minutes before serving, stir in the tomato paste and adjust the seasoning to taste.

Serve with fluffy basmati rice or quinoa and a cool leafy salad.

Notes:

RAPADURA SUGAR is an unrefined sugar made from evaporated sugar cane juice and can be purchased from most supermarkets.

SOPA SECA (PERUVIAN PASTA BAKE)

SERVES 4–6

60 ml (1/4 cup) extra virgin olive oil, plus extra for greasing

500 g angel hair pasta, broken into 10 cm pieces

1 1/2 onions, chopped

5 garlic cloves, crushed

4 chipotles in adobo

600 g tinned whole tomatoes

1 1/2 teaspoons ground coriander

1 1/2 teaspoons dried oregano

2 fresh bay leaves

500 ml (2 cups) chicken-style vegan stock

400 g tinned black beans (or use whatever beans you have)

handful chopped coriander leaves, to serve

CORIANDER CASHEW CREAM – see next page

This amazing Peruvian pasta dish has been the most misunderstood item on the Smith & Daughters menu. The staff still beg us to bring it back. If you don't think of it as spaghetti bolognese, or anything Italian and pasta-y that you're used to, you're in for a real treat. It's totally delicious, spicy and unusual. Make it! See for yourself!

Preheat the oven to 170°C. Lightly grease a 30 cm x 20 cm ovenproof dish with olive oil.

Heat the extra virgin olive oil in a large saucepan over medium heat. Add the pasta and fry for 2–3 minutes until golden brown. Drain on paper towel.

Place the onion, garlic, chipotles, tomatoes, ground coriander and oregano in a blender and process until smooth. Transfer the sauce to a pan with the bay leaves and cook over medium heat for approximately 10 minutes, or until thickened.

Stir in the stock, fried pasta and beans, and season with salt and pepper, to taste.

Bring to the boil, then reduce the heat and simmer gently, uncovered, breaking up the pasta with a spoon, for about 5 minutes.

Remove the bay leaves, then transfer the mixture to the prepared ovenproof dish and cover loosely with foil. Bake for about 20 minutes, until most of the liquid has been absorbed.

SOPA SECA (PERUVIAN PASTA BAKE)

CORIANDER CASHEW CREAM

155 g (1 cup) raw cashews, soaked (we use broken cashew pieces which only have to be soaked for 1 hour, but if you can only find whole cashews, soak them for at least 5 hours)

juice of 1 lemon

1 tablespoon apple cider vinegar

large handful coriander, stalks and leaves roughly chopped

1 teaspoon salt

FOR THE CORIANDER CASHEW CREAM, rinse and drain the cashews, then place in a blender with the remaining ingredients and 170 ml (2/3 cup) cold water. Blend on medium speed for a few minutes until smooth. Add a little more water if you prefer a slightly thinner cream.

Serve sopa seca drizzled with coriander cashew cream and coriander leaves scattered over the top.

Notes:

LEFTOVER CORIANDER CASHEW CREAM – lucky you! Use it anytime a recipe calls for sour cream, or as a dip.

This is an edited extract from Smith & Daughters: A Cookbook (that happens to be vegan) *by Shannon Martinez and Mo Wyse, published by Hardie Grant Books RRP $48.00 and available in stores nationally.*

'WE HAVE THE CHOICE TO USE THE GIFT OF OUR LIVES TO MAKE THE WORLD A BETTER WORLD FOR ALL LIVING BEINGS.'

Dr. Jane Goodall

GIANT PASTA WITH MUSHROOM SAUCE

SERVES 2–4

250 grams large dry pasta, like rigatoni or penne

1 teaspoon salt, for the pasta water

1/2 large brown onion, finely diced

2 large cloves garlic, crushed

4 cups Swiss brown mushrooms, sliced (stalks and all)

1/3 cup dry white wine

1.5 cups rice milk

1 teaspoon porcini powder (optional, but amazing)

1 teaspoon cornflour

1 teaspoon chopped fresh rosemary

2 cups asparagus, woody ends removed, sliced

oil

salt and pepper, to taste

Notes:

NUTRITIONAL YEAST will add some 'cheesiness'. Stir through a tablespoon of flakes before serving.

I love this creamy yet dairy-free dish. It's warming, hearty, fragrant and nourishing, especially on cold days. When you sauté the mushrooms slowly, their full flavour is released, so don't get impatient and rush this part.

Bring a large pot of water to the boil with a teaspoon of salt.

Heat some oil in a pan. Add the onion and garlic and cook till the onion is caramelised.

Add a little more oil to the pan and sauté the mushrooms over medium heat until soft and nicely browned.

Add the white wine and deglaze the pan.

Add the rice milk and porcini powder to the mushroom mix and simmer gently.

In a small dish, mix the cornflour with enough water to combine to a watery consistency and stir till free of lumps. Add the cornflour mixture slowly to the mushroom mix, stirring until the sauce coats the back of a spoon. Add the asparagus and continue to gently simmer for another minute or so.

Stir the rosemary through and check the seasoning. Add salt and pepper to taste.

Cook pasta in boiling water till al dente. Strain the cooked pasta and add it to the mushroom sauce and stir gently till combined.

Serve with crusty bread.

ANNA WEATHERLAKE

SPAG BOL

1 teaspoon coconut oil

1 brown onion, chopped

1 large carrot, chopped

1 stalk celery, chopped

1 x 125 g can corn kernels

4 cloves garlic, crushed

400 g vegie mince (I use Vegie Delights Savoury Vege Mince)

1 x 400 g can diced tomatoes

1/2 cup vegetable stock

1/2 teaspoon ground nutmeg

1 cup spinach leaves

1/2 teaspoon salt

1/2 teaspoon black pepper

1/2 cup chopped parsley

black bean spaghetti, raw zucchini noodles or pasta of your choice, to serve

CASHEW PARMESAN

1/2 cup cashews

3 tablespoons nutritional yeast flakes

1/2 teaspoon garlic powder

One of my favourite meals to cook when I am run off my feet is this tasty plant-based alternative to the classic spaghetti bolognese. Using a vegie mince base with plenty of additional vegetables, plus a sprinkle of tasty cashew parmesan on top, it's a nutritious crowd pleaser that is quick and easy to prepare. Winner!

FOR THE CASHEW PARMESAN, blend all the ingredients in a food processor until a fine powder has formed. Set aside.

FOR THE BOLOGNESE, heat the coconut oil in a large saucepan and sauté the onion, carrot, celery, corn and garlic for approximately 5 minutes, or until onion is translucent.

Add the vegie mince, tomatoes, stock, nutmeg, spinach, salt and pepper and stir through. Simmer for approximately 15 minutes with the lid on, stirring occasionally.

Stir in the chopped parsley and remove from the heat. Serve with your choice of pasta or noodles and cashew parmesan.

LENTIL SHEPHERD'S PIE

SERVES 4–6

oil for cooking

1 large brown onion, finely diced

2–3 large cloves garlic, minced

2 cups grated unpeeled carrot, approx. 2 large carrots

2 cups finely sliced celery

1 teaspoon hot chilli powder

1 tablespoon ground cumin

1/2 tablespoon ground coriander

3 tablespoons curry powder

1 1/2 cups green/brown lentils, rinsed well

1 x 400g can crushed tomatoes

5 cups vegetable stock

1 teaspoon salt

pepper to taste

1 bunch coriander, leaves only, washed and roughly chopped

MASHED POTATO – see next page

As a vegan, I enjoy a much more diverse diet, including almost everything I used to eat: pies, burgers, pizza, cheese, pasta, desserts and so on. Now I simply eat the plant-based version. I substitute the meat with beans, lentils, vegetables, nuts, jackfruit and so on. This shepherd's pie is delicious hearty food that your family and friends will love.

Gently heat a little oil in a large pot and sauté the onion till softened. Add the garlic and stir for another minute or two. Add the carrot and celery and cook for 5 minutes.

Dry roast the spices in a small pan on low heat for a minute or two to bring out their fragrance, stirring frequently.

Add the spices, lentils, tomatoes and stock to the pot and stir to combine. Bring it all to the boil, then turn the heat down to a very gentle simmer. Cook the lentils, uncovered, till they are tender, approximately 45 minutes. Add a little extra stock if you need to, but you don't want the lentil mix to be too watery or the mashed potato will blend in rather than sit on top.

Preheat the oven to 180°C.

LENTIL SHEPHERD'S PIE

MASHED POTATO

3–4 large potatoes, peeled and cut into small cubes (approx. 6 cups)

1/4 cup plant-based milk, such as almond or rice milk

FOR THE MASHED POTATO, bring a large pot of water to the boil. Cook the potatoes until tender, then drain and add the milk. Mash it all together till you get a nice smooth consistency. Add a little extra milk if you need to. Season well with the salt and add pepper to taste.

Once the lentils are ready, stir the fresh coriander through and spread evenly into a baking dish. Allow to cool a little.

Spread the mashed potato over the lentils and bake for about 15 minutes, or until the potato starts to brown.

Notes:

POTATOES: use any type that is good for mashing. The smaller you cut up the potatoes, the quicker they will cook.

LENTILS: If you use different lentils, they will take either more or less time to cook depending on which ones you choose. This will affect how much stock you need and the overall flavour of the dish.

SAUTÉ THE ONION in a little water for a change. You'll find that with many dishes like this you just don't need the oil.

SERVES 6

oil, for frying

1 small onion, finely diced

1 leek, sliced

1 cup pumpkin, finely chopped

100 g vegan margarine (we use Butter Me Up)

1 litre soy milk

4 tablespoons nutritional yeast

1x 300g silken tofu

1–2 teaspoons chicken style stock powder (we use Massels)

2 cloves garlic, crushed, or 1 teaspoon garlic powder

salt and pepper, to taste

1/4 cup chopped chives

1 tablespoon cornflour

200g uncooked pasta of your choice

handful of fresh breadcrumbs

parsley, chopped, for garnish

salad, to serve

Notes:

CRISPY FRIED VEGAN BACON can be added if you like. Add it either before baking or sprinkled on top. There are many mock bacon products on the market now – find the one you like best.

CHEEZY MAC

When we first became vegan, I was worried about how I would cope without butter. Cheese came a close second. Now I don't miss dairy at all, and I'm happy knowing that I don't support the dairy industry in any way. Sam's Cheezy Mac is delicious, real hearty comfort food without a dairy product in sight!

Preheat the oven to 180°C.

Heat a little olive oil in a pan and fry onion, leek and pumpkin on medium heat until soft. Try not to brown the vegies.

Add the vegan margarine, stock, garlic, nutritional yeast and tofu. Blend the cornflour with a little soy milk, and stir into the mixture. Add remaining soy milk and stir until everything is well combined. Cook for 5–10 minutes then blend until smooth and creamy.

Cook pasta according to instructions, till al dente.

Check sauce seasoning, adding salt and pepper to taste, and stir through chopped chives. Combine with cooked pasta in an ovenproof dish. Scatter the breadcrumbs over the top, drizzle with olive oil and bake for 15–20 minutes or until brown and bubbling.

Sprinkle with some chopped parsley and serve with a green salad.

HALF PINT VEGAN DAIRY

Sam Colligan & Jules Donovan

Jules's last words as a dairy eater were, 'But what am I going to do without butter?' Sam, a chef, pledged to make her a vegan butter, which then led to starting Half Pint Vegan Dairy. Through developing delicious products like Butter Me Up and vegan ice-cream for their own use, Sam and Jules realised that they couldn't possibly be the only ones who didn't want to eat margarine – other vegans must want these too. There was a gap in the market just waiting to be filled.

Before becoming vegan, Jules and Sam were both on-and-off vegetarians, then committed conscious vegetarians. They transitioned from shopping at farmers' markets, buying free-range meat and then biodynamic free-range, before saying, 'Actually, none of this is acceptable. We'd order organic free-range turkey for Christmas and think we were doing the right thing. But the animal had to die and that's not OK,' Jules explained.

Sam is a researcher; once she starts to question something, she finds the facts and makes up her mind. She realised that eating dairy was just as bad ethically as eating meat, and her decision to become vegan was lightning-bolt fast. Jules took a couple of months longer, but once she was armed with the facts, butter didn't matter so much anymore.

Their path to being vegan was an ethical progression, one that also included trying to shop locally, and choosing products that used less packaging. Jules's interest in animal welfare started with a rescue dog thirty years ago, and her

Jules, Beethoven and Sam

decision to become vegan is very much an environmental one too. 'Without the planet, those animals don't have anywhere to live. It's all connected: think about what you're doing and the impact it has.'

Jules has a great piece of advice: 'Here's the lazy version of being ethical. By choosing to be vegan, I only have to do one thing to save the entire planet, the human race and all the animals! Everything flows on from that one decision. I am saving water, I am saving energy, but I only have to think about being vegan.'

Sam's biggest challenge in becoming vegan has been realising that people she loved, admired and respected didn't care about the same issues. 'When something has become so astoundingly obvious yet other people can't see it, it's hard to understand,' she says.

After three years of hard work, and eighteen months before that developing the range, Jules and Sam have taken a break from Half Pint and the challenges of delivering a handmade product to retailers. They're thinking about the next move. 'We had lovely demand, but there are other people now doing what we were doing, and we're taking the time to enjoy all those other products on the market.'

On choosing to be vegan, Jules says, 'Just do it. It's easier than you think. If you allow yourself to feel compassion in that way, it's incredibly rewarding.'

halfpintvegandairy.com.au

CALZONI FRITTI

MAKES 8

50 ml olive oil, plus extra for frying calzoni

1/2 small onion, finely diced

4 bunches English spinach, leaves picked and washed, stems discarded

salt

DOUGH

pea-sized ball of fresh yeast, or 2 teaspoons instant dried yeast

615 g double zero flour, plus extra for dusting

15 g salt

ALMOND AND CASHEW RICOTTA

3/4 cup almonds, soaked overnight

3/4 cup cashews, soaked overnight

1 cup unsweetened cold-pressed almond milk

salt and pepper

TOMATO SAUCE

1 x 400 g can Italian peeled tomatoes (preferably San Marzano tomatoes)

salt

4 basil leaves

Fried calzoni are so versatile. Eaten on a plate with a fresh salad for dinner, or with your fingers, al fresco style, they are simply delicious – especially when you get creative with the fillings! This recipe is one of our all-time faves. We recommend starting the night before to prepare the dough and to get the nuts soaking for the almond and cashew ricotta.

FOR THE DOUGH, dissolve the yeast in 370 ml lukewarm water. Add half the flour, mix well, add the salt and then mix in the rest of the flour. Knead until dough is smooth and elastic (about 10 minutes). Cover with a damp cloth and rest on the kitchen bench for 2 hours.

Divide the dough into eight pieces and roll into balls. Flour the base of a large container and place balls of dough inside, leaving enough space in between for each ball to double in size. Prove for 8–12 hours, or until doubled.

FOR THE ALMOND AND CASHEW RICOTTA, place soaked nuts and almond milk in a high-speed blender, season with salt and pepper (be generous with the pepper), and blend to a smooth, creamy consistency.

FOR THE TOMATO SAUCE, hand-crush the tomatoes with salt to taste. Tear up the basil leaves and add to the sauce.

CALZONI FRITTI

FOR THE FILLING, heat the olive oil in a saucepan and sauté the onion until lightly golden. Add the spinach leaves and sauté until just wilted and any water has evaporated. Season with salt and remove from the heat.

TO MAKE THE CALZONI, use a scraper to remove the dough balls from the container, making sure to keep them round.

Flour the bench and the dough balls. Take a ball and, using your fingers, press firmly against the dough to form a disc. Pull the edges of the dough out to enlarge the disc to approximately 20 cm in diameter, being careful not to make any holes (to avoid oil getting in when calzoni are fried). Repeat with remaining dough balls.

Spread a tablespoonful of almond and cashew ricotta over half of each disc, leaving enough space (approx. 2 cm) to fold over and seal. Follow with the spinach mixture, dividing evenly between the discs.

Fold the other side of the dough over and press firmly around the edge to seal the ingredients inside each calzone.

Fill a saucepan with olive oil to about 5 cm and heat to 180°C. Fry calzoni in batches on both sides until golden brown.

Drain on paper towel to remove excess oil, drizzle with tomato sauce and enjoy!

SUPERGREEN PIZZA

SERVES 4

1 bunch broccolini

1 zucchini, thinly sliced

extra virgin olive oil, for roasting and to serve

4 zucchini flowers, quartered

toasted pepitas, to serve

mixed micro herbs and flowers, to serve

zest of 1 lemon, to serve

PESTO

90 g pepitas

1 teaspoon finely chopped garlic

1 small bunch kale (300 g), roughly chopped

2 handfuls of baby spinach leaves

1 bunch basil, leaves picked

juice of 1 lemon

1 teaspoon salt

100 ml extra virgin olive oil, plus extra to adjust consistency, if needed

DOUGH – see next page

This is a fresh and healthy pizza without the need for any dairy, but also works well with vegan mozzarella or parmesan. Start the dough two days ahead of time – yes, two! Trust us, as soon as you bite into the perfectly crispy, chewy crust, you'll see why.

FOR THE DOUGH, place the ingredients in the bowl of a stand mixer with a dough hook. Turn on the mixer and gradually add 390 ml water, mixing until the dough has come together, about 10 minutes. Place the dough in an oiled bowl, cover with plastic wrap and refrigerate for 48 hours.

Two to four hours before you are ready to eat, remove the dough from the fridge, shape into four balls and leave to rise in a warm place until doubled in size.

FOR THE PESTO, process the pepitas and garlic in a food processor, followed by the kale, spinach, basil and lemon juice. Gradually pour in the olive oil, adding more if necessary until the pesto reaches an easily spreadable consistency. Season with the salt.

FOR THE TOPPING, preheat the oven to 180°C.

Bring a small saucepan of water to the boil and cook the broccolini for 2 minutes, until just tender and bright green. Blanch in iced water, drain, chop roughly and set aside.

Drizzle the zucchini slices with olive oil and cook in the oven until lightly roasted. Set aside.

DOUGH

600 g good quality 00 pizza flour

2 1/2 teaspoons salt

1 teaspoon instant dried yeast

FOR THE PIZZA, place pizza stones, if you have them, or baking trays in the oven and increase the heat to the highest possible setting.

Knock the air from the dough and stretch out the pizza bases on a lightly floured surface (see note). Spread generously with pesto and top with zucchini slices and flowers and chopped broccolini. Slide onto the pizza stones or trays and transfer to the oven, being careful not to leave the door open for too long as a high temperature is crucial for a crispy base.

Cook until pizza bases are cooked through and golden brown. Remove from the oven and scatter with toasted pepitas, micro herbs and flowers, and lemon zest. Finish with a drizzle of olive oil and serve.

Notes:

WE COOK OUR PIZZA AT 400°C, but most home ovens won't go this high.

STRETCH THE DOUGH BY HAND, if you can, rather than using a rolling pin, if you're after a nice thin base with a bubbly crust like ours. We know it's easier at home to use a rolling pin but give it a go stretching by hand.

USE A MIX OF FLOUR AND POLENTA, if you like, for the floured surface.

PUMPKIN PIZZA

MAKE AS MANY AS YOU WANT!

pumpkin, peeled and thinly sliced

wholemeal pizza base of your choice (see note)

crushed tomatoes

onion, sliced

olives

vegan almond feta, crumbled

vegan soy cheese, grated

sesame seeds

This is one of the most popular pizzas on the menu at Nostralis. The roasted pumpkin brings great taste and colour to the pizza, and complements the vegan feta perfectly. We follow our hearts when we're piling on the toppings, and encourage you to do the same – use as much of each ingredient as you like.

Preheat the oven to 180°C.

Place pumpkin slices on a baking tray lined with baking paper and roast until soft and golden. Remove pumpkin from the oven. Put pizza stone or baking tray in the oven, and turn the heat up as high as it will go.

Spread crushed tomatoes over pizza base and cover with pumpkin slices, then layer the sliced onion, olives and vegan feta on top.

Finally, cover with soy cheese and top with a sprinkle of sesame seeds.

Transfer to floured pizza stone or baking tray and bake in the oven for 10–12 minutes, until crust is golden brown and cheese is melted. (This is based on a temperature of 220°C.)

Cut up and enjoy!

Notes:

SOY CHEESE AND VEGAN ALMOND FETA can be purchased from online vegan food suppliers. We use Cheezly brand.

MEXICANA PIZZA

MAKE AS MANY AS YOU WANT!

dried borlotti beans, soaked overnight in plenty of cold water (or use canned borlotti beans)

wholemeal pizza base of your choice (to make your own, see instructions below)

crushed tomatoes

green capsicum, sliced

onion, sliced

vegan soy cheese, grated

chilli flakes

The perfect pizza for spice lovers! The chilli goes very well with the borlotti beans, so add as much as you like, plus any extra vegies that you fancy.

Rinse and drain the borlotti beans, place in a saucepan and cover with cold water. Bring to the boil and cook for 1–2 hours until tender. Drain and set aside.

Place pizza stone or baking tray in the oven and preheat to the highest possible temperature.

Grab your pizza base and cover with crushed tomatoes. Spread borlotti beans evenly over the base, then layer the sliced capsicum and onion on top.

Finally, cover with soy cheese and top with a sprinkle of chilli flakes for that extra kick.

Transfer to floured pizza stone or baking tray and bake in the oven for 10–12 minutes, until crust is golden brown and cheese is melted. (This is based on a temperature of 220°C.)

Notes:

FOR BORLOTTI BEANS, 1 cup dried beans will yield 2 1/2 cups when cooked.

MAKE YOUR OWN PIZZA DOUGH (enough for two 30 cm pizzas): combine 250 g organic wholemeal plain flour in a bowl with 1 x 7 g sachet of instant dried yeast and a pinch of salt. Add 175 ml lukewarm water and mix to form a dough. Knead by hand or in a stand mixer with dough hook attachment until dough is smooth and elastic. Transfer to an oiled bowl, cover and leave in a warm place until doubled in size. Divide dough into two portions, roll out and transfer to floured pizza trays or stones, ready for topping.

THE KINDNESS BURGER

SERVES 4

1 tablespoon coconut oil, plus extra for frying

1 teaspoon ground turmeric

1/2 teaspoon ground coriander

1/4 teaspoon cayenne pepper

200 g carrot, grated

200 g parsnip, grated

1 tablespoon apple cider vinegar

1 tablespoon olive oil

salt (we use Murray River salt)

cracked black pepper

100 g tricolour quinoa

1 teaspoon roughly chopped fresh thyme

4 tablespoons buckwheat flour, sifted

4 burger buns

tofu aioli, to serve – see page 48

fennel, red cabbage and carrot slaw, to serve – see page 80

sweet potato chips, to serve – see page 48

May we present ... The Kindness Burger, the go-to plant-power burger for vegans! Because when you can eat a healthy, nutritious and downright delicious burger without harming others, why wouldn't you?

Start the patties the day before – this will give the mixture time to bind.

Heat the coconut oil in a saucepan over medium heat, then add the turmeric, coriander and cayenne pepper, followed by the carrot and parsnip. Cook the vegetables down slowly for about 15 minutes, until soft but not overcooked. Add the vinegar and olive oil, as well as salt and pepper to taste, and keep slowly cooking and turning the mixture over.

Meanwhile, place the quinoa in a saucepan with 2 cups of cold filtered water and 1 teaspoon of salt. Bring to the boil then lower the heat and simmer for 5 minutes. Remove from the heat, then rest for another 5 minutes (the dark grains will be firmer than the white but that's okay as it gives the burger texture).

Drain quinoa thoroughly and introduce to the saucepan with the vegetable mixture and thyme. Bring the heat up to get rid of any excess water, then stir in the sifted flour. Remove from the heat and allow to rest in the saucepan for as long as possible.

THE KINDNESS BURGER

Transfer the mixture to a sealed container and refrigerate, overnight if possible.

Preheat the oven to 180°C and line a baking tray with baking paper. Form burger mixture into four patties with wet hands.

Heat a little coconut oil in a frying pan over medium heat and cook patties for about 3 minutes on each side, or until they get a lovely crispy golden crust. Place on the lined tray in the oven for 10 minutes to finish cooking.

Toast burger buns and spread on both sides with tofu aioli. Top with patties and coleslaw, and serve with sweet potato chips, if desired. Yum!

Notes:

GLUTEN-FREE BUNS from GF Precinct artisan bakers are our preference.

ETHIOPIAN SPICED SWEET POTATO BURGERS

SERVES 6

1 small brown onion, finely diced

1 clove garlic, finely diced

2 tablespoons canola oil

2 stalks kale, stems removed, leaves roughly chopped

2 large sweet potato (about 1.2 kg), peeled and cut into 3 cm pieces

1/2 cup split red lentils

1/4 cup chickpea (besan) flour

burger buns, sauce and salad, to serve

BERBERE SPICE BLEND

1 teaspoon cumin seeds

1 teaspoon coriander seeds

1/2 teaspoon whole black peppercorns

1/2 teaspoon fenugreek seeds

1/4 teaspoon ground ginger

1/4 teaspoon ground cloves

1/4 teaspoon ground nutmeg

1/4 teaspoon dried chilli flakes

1/2 teaspoon dried oregano

1 teaspoon salt

We love the Ethiopian berbere spice blend in these burgers. We make our own using freshly toasted whole seeds, but a good quality berbere mix can be used as a substitute.

FOR THE BERBERE SPICE BLEND, toast the whole spices in a dry pan over low heat until fragrant (3–5 minutes). Coarsely grind the toasted spices in a mortar and pestle (or spice grinder), mix in the remaining spices, herbs and salt, and set aside.

FOR THE PATTIES, preheat the oven to 180°C.

In a large frying pan, cook the onion and garlic over low–medium heat with a little oil until soft but not coloured. Add the chopped kale leaves and continue to cook on low heat for 1–2 minutes until slightly softened.

Add the sweet potato and spice blend, tossing to combine. Transfer the mixture to an ovenproof dish and bake for 30–40 minutes, stirring occasionally, until the sweet potato is soft.

Meanwhile, put the lentils in a small saucepan with 1½ cups cold water. Cover and bring to the boil over medium heat. Turn down the heat and simmer for 5–7 minutes until lentils are soft. Drain and set aside.

When the sweet potato is cooked, remove from the oven (but don't turn the oven off) and allow to cool slightly before

ETHIOPIAN SPICED SWEET POTATO BURGERS

transferring to a bowl and mashing roughly. Add the lentils and chickpea flour, and mix well to combine using a large spoon or your hands.

Form mixture into 6 patties, depending on how thick you like your burgers, and place gently on a baking tray lined with baking paper. Bake for 20–25 minutes, or until slightly crusty on top.

TO ASSEMBLE, toast burger buns and top with salad, sauce of your choice and sweet potato patties.

Notes:

BERBERE SPICE BLENDS VARY. If you don't make your own, add 4–5 teaspoons of a bought blend, depending on the level of heat.

A BURGER WITH THE LOT – that's what we like. Add smashed avocado, spinach leaves, tomato, carrot, tomato kasundi or relish, and sprouts.

MAPLE BACON BURGER

SERVES 4

generous 1/3 cup (75 g) brown rice

1/2 tablespoon sea salt, plus extra to season

1 tablespoon sunflower oil, plus extra for frying

1 cup chopped white onion

1 clove garlic, chopped

2 tablespoons sunflower seeds

1/2 cup (27 grams) chopped sweet potato

1/4 cup (25 grams) finely cubed portobello mushrooms (make sure you remove the stems first)

1/2 teaspoon coarsely ground black pepper

2 tablespoons chopped spring onion

1 tablespoon chia seeds, ground in a spice grinder or mortar and pestle

1/2 cup (85 grams) canned adzuki beans, drained and rinsed

1 teaspoon dried basil

1 tablespoon chickpea (besan) flour

more ingredients over page >>

This is the most popular item on our menu and my personal favourite. There's something so cheeky about having 'bacon' in a plant-based restaurant. The coconut bacon is so good, it's dangerous. I'm careful these days not to make too much of it when I cook at home because I end up eating the leftovers.

Preheat the oven to 160°C.

FOR THE COCONUT BACON, toss the coconut, maple syrup, coconut aminos, salt, sunflower oil and 1 tablespoon liquid smoke together in a mixing bowl.

Spread the coconut mixture evenly over a baking tray lined with baking paper and cook in the oven until brown and toasted – approximately 10–15 minutes.

Transfer mixture to a bowl, add the remaining liquid smoke and stir through. Set aside.

FOR THE BURGER PATTIES, combine the rice and salt in a saucepan with 1½ cups water. Bring to the boil, then lower the heat, cover and simmer until all the liquid has been absorbed.

Process the cooked rice in a food processor using the pulse button. Be careful not to over-process the mixture – it should look like crushed rice.

MAPLE BACON BURGER

1/2 tablespoon maple extract

1/2 tablespoon maple syrup

4 vegan brioche burger buns

1/3 cup vegan mayonnaise

4 butterhead lettuce leaves

1 tomato, sliced

1 onion, sliced

2 dill pickles, chopped

COCONUT BACON

2 cups dried coconut flakes or shaved coconut

1 1/2 tablespoons maple syrup

1 1/2 tablespoons coconut amino sauce

1/2 tablespoon sea salt

1/2 tablespoon sunflower oil

2 tablespoons liquid smoke

Heat the sunflower oil in a saucepan and add the onion, garlic, sunflower seeds, sweet potato and mushrooms. Season with the pepper and salt to taste and cook until the sweet potato is soft.

Add the spring onion, ground chia seeds and adzuki beans and incorporate well with a wooden spoon. When the sweet potato is cooked through, take the saucepan off the heat and allow to cool.

In a large bowl, combine the cooked rice, dried basil, chickpea flour, maple extract and syrup and sweet potato mixture. Mix well, then mould into four patties with wet hands.

Heat a large non-stick frying pan over medium–high heat and fry patties in sunflower oil until golden brown on both sides and cooked through.

TO ASSEMBLE BURGERS, toast the brioche buns in a skillet or frying pan. Spread bottom buns with vegan mayonnaise, add a lettuce leaf, two tomato slices, two onion rings (or to taste), burger patty, chopped pickle and then the coconut bacon. Spread some more mayo on the top bun and voila – deliciousness.

Notes:

COCONUT AMINO SAUCE can be found in health food stores.

MAPLE EXTRACT AND LIQUID SMOKE can be found in gourmet and specialty grocery stores.

EXTRA COCONUT BACON can be stored in an airtight jar, ready for your next maple bacon burger. You can add it as a tasty flavouring to salads.

SERVES 6

3 x 300 g packets tempeh, cut into matchsticks

2 x 180 g packets smoked tofu, cut into matchsticks

2 tablespoons chipotle paste

2 tablespoons chilli sauce

2 tablespoons caramelised onion

6 dill pickles, sliced

1/2 cup pickled jalapeños, sliced

1 tablespoon smoked paprika

roasted red pepper

salt and pepper

olive oil, for cooking and drizzling

vegan cheese, grated (as much or as little as you like – you be the judge!)

6 x crusty rolls

baby spinach leaves

sliced red onion

coleslaw

bean shoots

coriander leaves

chips and/or salad, to serve, optional

CHIPOTLE AIOLI – see next page

PULLED TEMPEH ROLL WITH CHIPOTLE AIOLI

Here it is, one of our most popular dishes: the pulled tempeh roll! This 100 per cent cruelty-free classic packs in the flavour and pairs remarkably well with a good cold beer, we're told …

MAKE CHIPOTLE AIOLI (see next page).

Place the tempeh and smoked tofu in a mixing bowl, along with the chipotle paste, chilli sauce, caramelised onion, pickles, jalapeños, smoked paprika and roasted red pepper. Season with salt and pepper and fold ingredients together to combine. Be gentle as the tempeh and tofu are pretty easy to break.

Heat up a hotplate or frying pan and cook tempeh mix in a little olive oil, turning gently, until heated through. Sprinkle generously with grated vegan cheese.

While the cheese is melting, toast the bread and drizzle with olive oil. Fill rolls with spinach, sliced onion, tempeh mix, chipotle aioli and coleslaw, with bean shoots and coriander on top. Serve with chips and/or salad on the side, if desired.

PULLED TEMPEH ROLL WITH CHIPOTLE AIOLI

CHIPOTLE AIOLI

1 small jar of your favourite vegan mayonnaise

chipotle paste, to taste

crushed garlic, to taste

salt and pepper

FOR THE CHIPOTLE AIOLI, mix all the ingredients together, tasting as you go to get the right balance of heat from the chipotle paste and garlic. Set aside.

Notes:

TEMPEH (pressed, fermented soy beans) and smoked tofu can be purchased from health food stores and Asian grocers.

TO CARAMELISE ONIONS, slice and cook in olive oil with a good pinch of salt over a medium heat, stirring frequently, until soft and golden (about 15 minutes). Reduce heat to low, add sugar, balsamic vinegar, salt and pepper to taste and continue cooking until dark and caramelised (another 15 minutes or so). Leftover caramelised onion will keep covered in the fridge for a couple of weeks.

THE ROLLS can be replaced with baguette or French stick, cut into roll-sized portions, enough to serve 6 people.

THE KIND COOK

Melanie Baker

My life changed seven years ago after a Mother's Day fun run. I was with my young son, and we were lured by a cow – or more specifically, by Kyle from Edgar's Mission wearing a cow suit – in Federation Square. I took a pamphlet from Pam Ahern and the rest is history. I went home and sat at my computer and researched everything I was eating, wearing, using and doing that involved animals. I had no idea how I was going to execute this plan but veganism became the only option.

I was shocked by what I found out about the dairy industry. People are often surprised to hear that it wasn't meat that made me vegan. The plight of dairy cows is so deeply hidden, masked by happy cow images on all dairy products. To me, the dairy industry has the cruelest practices.

A friend said to me once, 'Hearing you talk now and discovering all the pieces of the puzzle of your life ... it's like you were always going to be vegan.' Looking back, I can see that there probably is a clear path, starting with feeling nauseous at the smell of Mum's roasts when I was fourteen. I didn't know any vegetarians, but by the time I was in my early twenties I didn't really eat red meat at all.

After a while, being vegan became my new normal. Now I read ingredients, select vegan-friendly eateries, abstain when nothing is available and always carry snacks with me – it's a way of life. My husband isn't vegan, but our household is. I teach my son the lessons that Edgar's

Mission has taught me by giving a voice to animals – that like us, animals fiercely love and protect their families, form friendships, understand what's going on around them, feel joy, feel fear and feel pain.

I started The Kind Cook as a hobby of sorts. It gave me somewhere to share my newfound fervour for plant-based cooking, along with the importance of eating a wide variety from the plant world and how healing that can be. I realised fairly quickly that it was also a conduit for helping others who found themselves struggling with the basics, especially in the early stages of becoming vegan. The thrill when someone discovers a cake recipe for their vegan daughter on my website or a meal that becomes a family favourite is indescribable. There's nothing like celebrating a special occasion with something delicious that is simple to make, surprising someone you love with a tasty meal, or nourishing your family. Being vegan doesn't mean losing your love of good food!

My decision to become vegan is reinforced every day, the more I learn about the environmental impact of animal agriculture, the countless resources taken up by raising animals for consumption and how that affects our world where people are literally starving to death.

Now, I simply don't know any other way to live.

thekindcook.com

SWEET TREATS

small bites
slices
cakes
desserts

MAKES 14 LARGE DOUGHNUTS

125 ml soy milk

11 g egg replacer

800 g bakers (strong) flour

45 g sugar

29 g instant dried yeast

20 g salt

1 tablespoon bread improver

180 g vegetable shortening (something spreadable like a vegan margarine, not crumbly like coconut oil or copha)

approx. 2 litres sunflower oil

semolina, to dust

SMOKED MAPLE ICING

70 ml smoked maple syrup (to make your own, see next page)

1 teaspoon good quality flaked salt (we use Murray River pink salt)

40 g vegetable shortening, melted

360 g icing sugar

CANDIED PECANS

30 g salt

200 g pecans

150 g icing sugar

SMOKED MAPLE DOUGHNUTS

We make a new flavour of vegan doughnut pretty much every week but this one is easily the most popular. If you're not up to sourcing or making smoked maple syrup, they are still delicious with standard high quality maple syrup. Try using just about any other nut, or adding spices such as cinnamon to the dough – just add 20 g at the start of mixing. Over to you!

FOR THE DOUGHNUTS, pour the soy milk and 380 ml cold water into the bowl of a stand mixer and whisk in the egg replacer.

Add the flour, sugar, yeast, salt, bread improver and half of the vegetable shortening and mix on slow for 8 minutes. Add the remaining shortening and continue mixing for a further 6 minutes. If at either step the shortening is not completely absorbed, continue mixing until it is.

Place the dough in a lightly oiled bowl, cover with a tea towel and rest on the bench for 30 minutes, then refrigerate until the dough feels cold all the way through and has stiffened slightly. Knock the air out of the dough and return to the fridge for an hour.

Turn the dough onto a lightly floured bench and roll to approximately 15 mm thick. Cut out doughnuts with a doughnut cutter (or use a large ring cutter and remove

SMOKED MAPLE DOUGHNUTS

Notes:

MAKE YOUR OWN SMOKED MAPLE SYRUP

Soak a handful of apple (or similar) woodchips in water for at least 20 minutes. Make a small aluminium foil nest for the woodchips and place in the bottom of a wok. Drain the woodchips and place in the foil.

Sit a round wire cooling rack over the woodchips (ideally this will be large enough not to touch the chips but a little contact is okay). Place approx. 80 ml maple syrup in a small metal bowl on top of the wire rack and cover the wok.

Place the wok over high heat until it starts to smoke, then turn heat down to medium–low. It should keep smoking, but if it stops turn the heat up slightly. Smoke for approximately 15–20 minutes (longer if you're making a larger batch). Check the flavour if you're unsure – it should taste like a maple campfire.

Remove the bowl of syrup from the wok and cool slightly before proceeding with recipe.

the centres with a smaller one). Place doughnuts on a tray lightly dusted with semolina to prevent them sticking. Spritz lightly with water and prove at room temperature until they have roughly doubled in size.

About half an hour before the end of the proving time, prepare the toppings.

FOR THE SMOKED MAPLE ICING, combine all the ingredients in a large bowl, whisking until no lumps are present. The icing should be thick enough that when you draw a line through it with a knife it stays visible for 30 seconds; if it doesn't, add more icing sugar until it does. If your icing is too sweet, add more salt to taste.

FOR THE CANDIED PECANS, half-fill a small saucepan with water, add the salt and bring to the boil. Add the pecans and continue to boil for 1 minute.

Drain the pecans, allow to cool briefly and then toss in icing sugar to coat.

Fill a deep frying pan halfway with remaining sunflower oil and heat to a steady 180°C (the temperature is important so use a digital kitchen thermometer).

Fry the pecans in the hot oil for 5 minutes, then remove with a slotted metal spoon and place on a tray lined with baking paper, gently using the spoon to break apart large clumps. Set aside to cool.

In the same 180°C oil, fry the doughnuts three at a time for 2½ minutes each side. Use the slotted spoon to transfer them to a wire rack set over a tray to drain the excess oil.

Warm the icing until it has thinned slightly and dip the semolina side of the doughnuts in. Sprinkle with pecans immediately, before the icing dries. Enjoy!

PEANUT BUTTER COOKIES

MAKES ABOUT 24

280 g (1 cup) crunchy natural peanut butter

115 g (1/3 cup) rice malt syrup

1 teaspoon natural vanilla extract

50 g (1/3 cup) cornflour

1 teaspoon baking powder

100 g dark chocolate (70–85% cocoa solids), chopped into chunks

70 g (1/2 cup) roasted salted peanuts

These cookies are a dream come true for fans of peanut butter. As a bonus, they're gluten free. Make sure you buy peanut butter made from 100 per cent peanuts and organic if possible. Give it a good stir before you measure out the peanut butter, especially if the oil has separated. This recipe is one of my favourites.

Preheat the oven to 180°C (160°C fan-forced). Line two baking trays with non-stick baking paper.

Combine the peanut butter, rice malt syrup and vanilla extract in a large bowl. Add the cornflour and baking powder and mix well. Stir in the chocolate and peanuts until well combined. Using your hands may make this job easier.

Roll tablespoonfuls of the dough into balls and place on the prepared trays about 4 cm apart. Flatten the balls lightly with your fingertips to about 1.5 cm thick. Poke in any peanuts or bits of chocolate left behind in the bowl. Bake for 8–10 minutes or until just starting to colour around the edges. Remove from the oven and cool on the trays for 10 minutes. Transfer to wire racks to cool completely.

Store in an airtight container for up to a week.

This recipe is from Incredible Bakes (That Just Happen to be Refined-Sugar Free) *by Caroline Griffiths published by Smith Street Books, RRP $39.99, available in stores nationally. With triple-tested recipes that are completely delicious, natural sweetness is added using whole fruits and, sometimes, other non-fructose sweeteners, including rice malt syrup, dextrose and stevia.*

MAKES 12–16 SLICES

2 cups nuts (we use brazil nuts)

1/2 cup cacao powder

pinch each of nutmeg and ground cloves

1/2 teaspoon cinnamon

1 teaspoon vanilla extract

pinch of salt

finely grated rind of 1 orange

3–4 drops food grade peppermint essential oil

20 pitted dates soaked in hot water for 15 minutes

1/4 cup goji berries

1/2 cup melted coconut oil

TOPPING

100 g cacao butter

1/2 cup coconut oil

1/2 teaspoon vanilla extract

1/3 cup agave or coconut nectar

Notes:

ORDINARY SUNDRIED DATES can also be used – about 3/4 cup.

PEPPERMINT ESSENTIAL OIL from doTERRA or Young Living works well.

CHOCOLATE GOJI SLICE

Our idea of heaven is a raw vegan café … here's a recipe for one of our raw sweet treats so you can make a slice of heaven at home. We provide raw and vegan food and education that is affordable to everyone. Not to mention delicious!

Grind nuts in processor, add cacao, spices, vanilla, salt, orange rind and peppermint oil, then dates, and pulse until combined. Lastly add goji berries and the melted coconut oil, stirring through by hand.

Press mix into a 20 cm square tin lined with baking paper. Make sure that the surface is quite flat.

Refrigerate while you prepare the topping.

Melt cacao butter and coconut oil together. You can do this by placing them in a small metal bowl, and placing this bowl in a larger bowl that contains some boiling water. Once this mix is completely melted, add vanilla extract and the agave or coconut nectar. Whisk together and pour over the base. Making sure it's sitting flat, refrigerate for at least an hour or until the topping has hardened. Cut into squares.

The slice will keep in a sealed container in the refrigerator for at least a week.

PEANUT BARS

MAKES ABOUT 26 SMALL BARS

500 g pitted dates

780 g roasted peanuts

70 g coconut oil

1/2 teaspoon salt (we use Himalayan salt)

CHOCOLATE GANACHE

150 g coconut oil, melted

90 ml agave syrup

90 g raw cacao

pinch of salt

1 teaspoon vanilla bean seeds

Warning: This little treat is highly addictive. Enjoy responsibly and don't forget to share with friends!

Blend dates and 500 g peanuts in a food processor for 3 minutes until finely chopped enough to cling together when pressed. Transfer to a large bowl, add the remaining peanuts, coconut oil and salt and mix with clean hands until well combined.

Form the mixture into small bars (approximately 50 g) and freeze for 10–15 minutes.

While the bars are in the freezer, make the chocolate ganache. Blend all the ingredients for 5 seconds, or mix with a fork until smooth and well combined. If using a blender, take care not to overwork the mixture as the coconut oil may split.

Remove the bars from the freezer and dip into the ganache. Place on a tray lined with baking paper. Leave for 5 minutes to set before serving.

Notes:

THE MIXTURE can also be pressed into a 30 x 25 cm tray lined with baking paper extended over the two long sides. Freeze for 10-15 minutes. Cut into bars and return to the freezer before dipping.

THE GANACHE MIXTURE can be poured into ice-cube trays and allowed to set to make delicious individual chocolates. Just an idea!

RASPBERRY & CHOCOLATE MACARONS

MAKES 20 MACARONS

300 ml water drained from canned chickpeas (approx. 2 cans' worth)

MACARONS

100 g caster sugar

100 g almond meal, sieved

100 g icing sugar, sieved

30 g freeze-dried raspberry powder

25 g glucose syrup

DARK CHOCOLATE FILLING

100 g good quality dark chocolate

pinch of salt

TO ASSEMBLE

150 g good quality dark chocolate

raspberry jam

At Sweet Studio we believe vegans should not miss out. In fact, vegan cuisine should mean … delicious! We're a chocolate and cake shop that specialises in delicious and we often have vegan desserts on our menu, but they are only there because of merit; the fact that they are suitable for vegans is a bonus. This recipe was developed by one of our talented pastry chefs, Alison Marshall. We don't make macarons normally, as we like to have a different product range to our competitors … But these are different and we hope you enjoy them. You need to start the recipe the day before you make the macarons.

FOR THE AQUAFABA, place the drained chickpea water in a small saucepan and reduce by half. Pour the mixture into a container and store covered in the fridge overnight to cool and thicken.

FOR THE DARK CHOCOLATE FILLING, start a couple of hours before the macarons. Chop the chocolate into very small pieces and place in a large stainless steel bowl.

Bring 100 ml water to the boil and pour it onto the chocolate. Stir well, slowly at first, with a whisk to bring the ganache together. Add the salt and continue to whisk until you have a smooth cream.

Leave the filling to set for a couple of hours at room temperature before transferring to a piping bag fitted with a small plain piping nozzle.

FOR THE MACARONS, preheat the oven to 120°C. Grease two 30 cm x 20 cm baking trays and line with baking paper.

Place 75 ml aquafaba in the bowl of a stand mixer with the whisk attached.

Pour 25 ml water into a small clean saucepan and add the caster sugar. Stir to a sandy texture and clean the insides of the pan with a wet pastry brush.

Mix the almond meal, icing sugar and raspberry powder together in a mixing bowl. Sieve the mixture into a large clean bowl and set aside.

Start to whisk the aquafaba on medium speed. At the same time, place the saucepan on the stove and heat the contents to a boil. Add the glucose syrup, and cook to 110°C (use a digital kitchen thermometer to accurately measure the temperature).

Turn the stand mixer up to high speed and continue to cook the syrup until it reaches a temperature of 118°C. Remove the pan from the heat and slowly pour the syrup into the mixing bowl at the side to avoid hitting the whisk. Continue to whisk on high speed until all the syrup is incorporated and the meringue mixture is cold, shiny and thick.

Fold one-third of the meringue into the dry ingredients and then carefully fold in the remainder. Mix until smooth and glossy then transfer into a piping bag fitted with a small plain piping nozzle.

Pipe 20 evenly spaced 3 cm-diameter discs onto each baking tray and leave at room temperature for 40 minutes to 1 hour to form a skin.

Bake for 15–20 minutes. Turn off the oven but leave the

macaron shells inside for a further 10 minutes to dry out.

Remove from the oven and allow to cool at room temperature.

TO ASSEMBLE, melt the dark chocolate and cool to 30°C.

Use a small palette knife to loosen the macaron shells from the baking paper, and turn each of them over onto a clean work surface.

Spoon 1/2 teaspoon raspberry jam onto the inside of half of the shells, then pipe a teaspoon-size amount of the chocolate filling on top of the jam. Sandwich the jam and chocolate halves with the remaining shells, pushing them together gently. Half dip each macaron in the melted dark chocolate and stand up on a clean tray.

Place in the fridge for 5 minutes to set the chocolate and serve immediately.

Notes:

AQUAFABA is another name for the liquid in which beans or chickpeas have been cooked. It has emulsifying and foaming properties, which makes it an excellent substitute for egg whites.

CHICKPEA WATER: we start with 300 ml to allow plenty of margin for error. It's hard to reduce 150 ml to exactly 75 ml.

FREEZE-DRIED RASPBERRY POWDER can be found at specialty and gourmet grocery stores.

MATCHA PANCAKES WITH DARK CHOCOLATE SAUCE

SERVES 2

1 cup gluten-free flour

2 teaspoons panela sugar

1 tablespoon matcha

2 teaspoons baking powder

1/2 teaspoon sea salt

1 tablespoon vegetable oil

1 3/4 cups cold water

oil, for cooking

CHOCOLATE SAUCE

200 g Callebaut 74% dark chocolate

100 ml full-fat coconut milk (we use Kara brand)

pinch of salt

Our mission is to help the earth to survive so that you can thrive ... so we're sharing one of our signature dishes. We love it because of how creative you can be with it. Partner these pancakes with anything and we guarantee the result will be delicious, and kind to the earth.

FOR THE PANCAKES, whisk together the flour, sugar, matcha, baking powder and salt until well combined and aerated. Make a well in the centre of the dry ingredients and lightly mix in the oil, then slowly add the water until you have a smooth batter.

Heat a non-stick pan to a medium heat, lightly oil the pan (this will help create that nice light brown colour we love). Using your favourite spoon, place some mixture in the pan. When you start to see bubbles, flip that guy over and cook for a further minute. Repeat until your mix is finished. Depending on how big you want your pancakes, you'll get 6 to 8 from this mixture.

FOR THE CHOCOLATE SAUCE, melt the chocolate over a double boiler. In a separate pot, bring the coconut milk to a simmer. Slowly add the milk to the chocolate. When combined, add the salt. If you want an extra choc hit, we recommend adding a teaspoon of Mork dark cacao powder.

MATCHA PANCAKES WITH DARK CHOCOLATE SAUCE

Stack the pancakes and pour the chocolate sauce over the top. Serve with whatever your heart desires – try them with your favourite fruits and ices. We serve them with different berry textures, nut crumbles, mint and lemongrass coconut ice-cream, pears, passionfruit, lychees … have a look at our Instagram for more ideas.

Notes:

MATCHA MAIDEN is our preferred matcha because of its high quality and full flavour.

SEA OR RIVER SALTS work best but any salt will do.

VEGETABLE OIL can be exchanged for any subtly flavoured oil you want.

ANY PLANT-BASED MILK can be used instead of water for a richer flavour.

CASHEW PARFAIT & COCONUT MUSK

SERVES 18–20

500 g raw cashews, soaked overnight

500 ml almond milk

300 ml agave syrup

300 ml raspberry puree

300 g cocoa butter, melted

3 vanilla beans, split and seeds scraped

1 teaspoon salt

3 tablespoons soy lecithin

lemon juice, to taste

fresh seasonal fruit and dark chocolate shavings, to serve

COCONUT MUSK ESPUMA

500 ml coconut cream

200 g musk powder

Think of this recipe as your new vegan dessert best friend. Smart, fun and easygoing, you'll want to introduce it to everyone you know. It's not hard to make but you will need a cream whipper or siphon gun with N2O cartridges for the coconut musk espuma (that's Spanish for foam) – told you it was fun!

FOR THE PARFAIT, blitz in a food processor the soaked cashews, almond milk, agave syrup, raspberry puree, melted cocoa butter, vanilla and salt. While continuing to process the mixture, add the soy lecithin one spoon at a time. Add lemon juice to taste.

Line 4-inch (or small) round fondant moulds with baking paper.

Pour the mixture into the moulds, three-quarters high, and set in the freezer overnight.

Thirty minutes before serving, remove parfaits from freezer and allow to soften at room temperature.

FOR THE COCONUT MUSK ESPUMA, place ingredients in a bowl and whisk together until well combined. Transfer mixture into a cream whipper and charge with two nitrous oxide bulbs.

Unmould parfaits and serve with fresh seasonal fruit, dark chocolate shavings and coconut musk espuma.

Notes:

MUSK POWDER can be bought at specialty gourmet stores, or substitute musk candy.

CREAM WHIPPERS and nitrous oxide bulbs can be purchased from specialty cooking equipment stores.

COCONUT GELATO

MAKES ABOUT 1.3 LITRES

500 ml coconut cream

500 ml full-fat soy milk

250 g glucose syrup

40 g caster sugar

1/4 teaspoon salt

Don't let the name fool you – we might be a gourmet plant-based burger joint, but we also know a thing or two about the sweeter things in life. Our coconut shakes are famous, thanks to this amazing gelato. We make it from scratch in house, and suggest you do, too. It's super easy and it will rock your world.

Combine coconut cream, soy milk, glucose syrup, sugar and salt in a saucepan and bring to the boil, stirring to melt the glucose syrup and dissolve the sugar.

Remove from the heat and allow to cool to room temperature (you can speed this up by stirring over an ice bath if you like). Cover and refrigerate until thoroughly chilled.

Pour into an ice-cream machine and churn until frozen. If you don't have an ice-cream machine you can freeze the mixture for 45 minutes, then pull it out, whisk thoroughly and return to the freezer, repeating the process up to six times until the ice crystals are small and uniform and the consistency is smooth.

Notes:

GLUCOSE SYRUP can be found in the baking aisle of most supermarkets.

PAPAYA, PINEAPPLE & BASIL GRANITA

SERVES 4

500 ml fresh pineapple juice

300 ml fresh papaya juice

4 tablespoons pure maple syrup

1 cup fresh basil leaves

The simplest ideas can be the tastiest! This takes 10 minutes to prepare, and uses just four ingredients. The flavours work their summer magic while the granita freezes, so it's ideal for making ahead if you're entertaining. If the pineapple is super sweet, you can leave out the maple syrup.

Gently wash the basil leaves and remove any hard stalks.

Place all the ingredients into a blender and blend until the basil leaves have roughly broken up. Be sure not to over-blend the mixture or the basil will break up too much and your mixture will become green.

Pour the mixture into two flat trays and place them into the freezer, making sure the trays are sitting flat.

After an hour or so, as the mixture begins to freeze, use a fork to carefully scrape any of the mixture that has started icing up. Continue doing this every 20–30 minutes until all the mixture is completely flaked. If you are not serving straight away, just place it into an airtight container in your freezer until you want to use it.

When you are ready to serve the granita, serve it in chilled glasses and eat it before it melts.

RED VELVET CAKE WITH BUTTERCREAM FROSTING

SERVES 8

2 medium beetroots

50 g good quality dark chocolate, or 4 tablespoons good quality cocoa powder

soy milk (or other plant milk)

2 cups plain flour

2 1/2 teaspoons baking powder

3/4 cup caster sugar

1/2 cup cooking oil or margarine

1 tablespoon vinegar

warm chocolate sauce, optional, to serve

FROSTING

1/3 cup margarine

2 teaspoons lemon juice (or plant milk)

1–1 1/2 cups icing sugar

soy milk (or other plant milk) to adjust consistency, if needed

Adapted from one of the most popular cakes of all time, our traditional red velvet cake is a favourite at our market food stalls in autumn and winter, when local beetroots are at their seasonal best. Beetroot is not only high in iron and vitamin C, but also jam-packed with magnesium, folate and potassium. Even better, using it in this recipe allows us to reduce the amount of sugar and helps retain much of the moisture during the baking process, making this cake soft, moist and decadent.

Wash, top and tail the beetroots, cut into pieces and boil until soft. Drain, puree and allow to cool. This can be done a day ahead – simply store beetroot puree in the fridge until required.

Transfer beetroot puree to a measuring jug.

If using dark chocolate, melt chocolate over a saucepan of simmering water or in the microwave, then add to beetroot puree. If using cocoa powder, mix it into the puree. Add enough soy milk to make 1½ cups of liquid.

Preheat the oven to 160°C fan-forced (180°C conventional) and line a 20 cm cake tin with baking paper.

Sift the plain flour into a mixing bowl, add the baking powder and caster sugar, and mix well with a wooden spoon.

Stir the oil (or margarine) and vinegar into the dry ingredients and then slowly pour in the chocolatey beetroot puree.

Mix well with a hand whisk or wooden spoon until batter is light and fluffy. (Do not use an electric mixer as over-beating will make the gluten in the flour become tough and the cake will flop.)

Pour the batter into prepared cake tin and gently tap the tin a couple of times on the kitchen bench to get rid of air bubbles.

Bake for 30 minutes, then start checking with a bamboo skewer inserted into the middle of the cake – if the skewer comes out clean, the cake is ready. If the cake is still runny in the middle, leave it in the oven at the same temperature, checking every 10 minutes until the skewer comes out clean.

Leave cake to cool in the tin for at least 20 minutes before turning out onto a wire rack. Cool for at least 3 hours on a cold day and longer if the room temperature is warm. Make sure the cake is completely cool before frosting.

FOR THE FROSTING, soften the margarine by beating with an electric mixer at low speed for a couple of minutes. Slowly add the lemon juice and beat until fluffy – this may take about 3 more minutes.

To prevent lumpy frosting (and a kitchen covered with flyaway icing sugar), sift in half of the icing sugar initially and beat at medium speed. If the frosting is too runny, add more icing sugar. If it seems hard and lumpy, add one teaspoon of plant milk at a time and whisk until frosting is a fluffy consistency and stays on the whisk.

Place the cake on a plate and spread generously with frosting. Allow to harden for 1 hour before serving.

Notes:

THE CAKE WILL KEEP, with or without frosting, in an airtight container for up to 3 days at room temperature and for 4 weeks in the freezer. Allow cake to thaw on the kitchen bench for approximately 4 hours before serving.

INSTEAD OF ICING the cake, you can serve it with a warm chocolate sauce.

CHEWY BROWNIE SKILLET COOKIES

SERVES 6

260 g rice malt or coconut syrup

30 g raspberries, pureed

150 g coconut butter (creamed coconut)

100 g almond butter

85 g buckwheat flour

30 g raw cacao

22 g tapioca starch

2 teaspoons gluten-free baking powder

55 g dried cranberries

coconut yoghurt or ice-cream, to serve

fresh berries, to serve

toasted hazelnuts, to serve

RASPBERRY CHIA COULIS

240 g frozen raspberries, thawed

1 tablespoon rice malt or coconut syrup

25 g chia seeds

We all love a good, warm, fudge-centred cookie, and this recipe reinvents that classic favourite for everyone to enjoy. You can whip up a batch of these cookies in no time for surprise guests, and not only are they vegan and refined-sugar free, but gluten free too. Not that any of your guests will be able to tell!

FOR THE COULIS, place all the ingredients in a bowl and mix gently. Refrigerate for at least 20 minutes.

FOR THE COOKIES, bring a saucepan of water to the boil and set a heatproof bowl on top. Place the syrup, raspberry puree, coconut butter and almond butter in the bowl and stir until all the ingredients melt together. Remove bowl from the heat.

Mix the flour, cacao, tapioca starch and baking powder together and add to the liquid mixture. Stir until just coming together but not fully combined. Add the cranberries and mix until well combined. Refrigerate for 10 minutes.

Preheat the oven to 180°C.

Wearing gloves to help stop the mixture sticking to your hands, roll the dough into six balls.

CHEWY BROWNIE SKILLET COOKIES

Lightly grease 6 x 10 cm ovenproof skillets. Place balls of dough in the skillets and bake for 12–15 minutes (12 minutes for soft fudgey cookies and 15 minutes for something a bit firmer).

Serve cookies straight from the oven with your favourite coconut yoghurt or ice-cream, a spoonful of raspberry chia coulis, fresh berries and some toasted hazelnuts for a delicious crunch.

Notes:

MOST OF THESE INGREDIENTS can be found in health food stores and the health food aisles of some supermarkets.

MAKE THE DOUGH ahead of time, for even quicker skillet cookies. Roll dough into balls and store in an airtight container in the fridge for up to two weeks.

CHOCOLATE BEETROOT CAKE WITH RASPBERRIES & AVOCADO CHOCOLATE ICING

SERVES 12

1 medium beetroot (150 g)

200 g raspberries, fresh or frozen

2 cups (240 g) almond meal

1/2 cup (80 g) brown rice flour

1/2 cup (80 g) buckwheat flour or maize flour

1/2 cup (60 g) cocoa or cacao powder

1 1/2 cups rapadura, or other unrefined sugar

1 teaspoon bicarbonate of soda

pinch of salt

2 tablespoons flaxmeal, soaked in 2/3 cup water or rice milk for 15–20 minutes

1 cup (250 ml) rice milk

1/2 cup (120 g) coconut oil

1 tablespoon vanilla extract

2 tablespoons lemon juice

1 teaspoon lemon zest

raw cacao, to serve, optional

AVOCADO CHOCOLATE ICING – see next page

I take my hat off to whoever decided that vegetables can hide in cakes! The combination in this recipe makes my tastebuds sing, and I have lost count of how many times I've made it. Now you too can enjoy the health benefits of beetroot, avocado, coconut oil, cacao and raspberries all married into one decadent, celebratory cake. What more could you ask for?

Preheat the oven to 180°C. Grease a 23 cm round springform tin and line with baking paper.

FOR THE CAKE, peel and finely grate beetroot. If using frozen raspberries, make sure they are completely thawed otherwise the cake won't bake properly. Mix the almond meal, flours, cocoa, sugar, bicarb and salt in a large bowl. In another large bowl, combine the soaked flaxmeal, rice milk, coconut oil, vanilla and lemon juice and zest. Mix the dry ingredients into the wet ones, then stir in the beetroot. Add the berries and mix through very gently.

Pour into the cake tin and bake for about an hour. You don't want to overbake this cake, so check after 45 minutes by inserting a knife in the middle – if it comes out clean, it's ready.

Leave cake in the tin for 15–30 minutes, then remove from the tin and allow to cool on wire rack before icing.

CHOCOLATE BEETROOT CAKE WITH RASPBERRIES & AVOCADO CHOCOLATE ICING

AVOCADO CHOCOLATE ICING

1 large very ripe avocado

1/4 cup (80 ml) coconut or maple syrup, plus extra to taste, if needed

1 generous dash of vanilla extract

pinch of salt

1/3 cup (35 g) raw cacao, sifted, plus extra to taste, if needed

1/4 cup (60 ml) rice milk

2 tablespoons coconut oil, optional

FOR THE ICING, blend all the ingredients to a smooth and creamy consistency. You will need to use a blender or a hand-held mixer; mixing it by hand won't create a smooth icing. Taste and add extra cacao and coconut syrup if necessary. Place in the fridge to firm up.

Cover cake with icing and dust with cacao, if desired, for an elegant finish.

Notes:

FLAXMEAL is the product left after pressing flaxseeds to get flaxseed oil. It's available from health food shops.

THIS CAKE IS SUPER VERSATILE. You can make it with mixed berries instead of raspberries, or leave the berries out of the batter altogether and use them as a garnish. You can also use a whole range of different oils such as grapeseed, olive, sunflower or macadamia instead of coconut. And for health-conscious guests, you can reduce the sugar to 1 cup and the cake will still taste great.

INSTEAD OF THE ICING, simply spread maple syrup over the cake when it comes out of the oven and dust with cacao. Voila! Mind you, avocado chocolate icing doubles as an awesome chocolate mousse and freezes well. Just saying …

'YOU PUT A BABY IN A CRIB WITH AN APPLE AND A RABBIT. IF IT EATS THE RABBIT AND PLAYS WITH THE APPLE, I'LL BUY YOU A NEW CAR.'

Harvey Diamond

PAVLOVA

SERVES 12

chickpea water (chilled), from a 400 g can of chickpeas

3/4 cup white sugar

3/4 teaspoon cream of tartar

berries, passionfruit pulp and shavings of dark chocolate, to serve

COCONUT CREAM

4 x 400 ml cans Trident coconut cream

100 g sugar

2 teaspoons vanilla essence

1/2 teaspoon guar gum

25 g agar agar

Notes:

INSTEAD OF COCONUT CREAM, serve with coconut yoghurt.

THE MERINGUES will keep for a few days in a sealed container.

This is our signature dessert, a veganised version of the great Australian favourite.

Preheat oven to 150°C.

FOR THE MERINGUES, whip the chickpea water (from a can of chilled chickpeas) in a food processor until it has soft peaks. Be patient, this might take 10 minutes. Add the sugar and cream of tartar and whip until sugar is dissolved and mixture forms stiff peaks.

Line a baking tray with baking paper and dollop mixture into 12 portions.

Turn oven down to 100°C and bake the meringues for one hour. They will be soft to touch, but harden on cooling.

FOR THE COCONUT CREAM, put 2 cans of coconut cream, sugar, vanilla, guar gum and agar agar in a pot over medium heat and bring to a simmer, until agar agar is melted. Transfer to a plastic container and cool in fridge.

Once set, chop into rough pieces, and put into a high speed blender. Add remaining 2 cans of coconut cream, blending until it resembles thick cream. Transfer to a metal bowl that is sitting in another bowl of ice. Hand whisk until the cream has fluffy peaks.

Serve as individual mini pavlovas, or pile up the meringues, layering with coconut cream, berries, passionfruit pulp and shavings of dark chocolate.

MANGO & LIME CHEESECAKE WITH A CHEWY CHOCOLATE ALMOND CRUST

SERVES 4

1 cup cashews

1/4 cup fresh mango flesh

1/4 cup coconut cream

4 tablespoons melted coconut oil

2 tablespoons fresh lime juice

zest from 2 limes

2 tablespoons pure maple syrup

2 pinches salt

1/4 cup mango flesh, blended, to serve

1/2 cup thinly sliced mango, to serve

CRUST

1/4 cup almonds

3 fresh dates, pitted

1 tablespoon raw cacao

This delicious cheesecake is quite rich, so you only need small slices. Double the base ingredients if your processor is going to struggle with such a small amount, and roll the extra mixture into balls to eat as a snack.

Use a springform tin (10 cm diameter and 7 cm depth), lightly sprayed with oil and then lined with baking paper.

FOR THE CRUST, blend the almonds, dates and cacao in a high powered blender until they are well combined and form a dough-like consistency. If the mixture is a little too dry, add a teaspoon of water to bring it together.

Press the crust into the base of the springform tin. It can be quite sticky so wet your fingers a little if you need to.

FOR THE FILLING, place the ingredients into a high powered blender or food processor. Blend until smooth.

Spoon the mixture onto the crust.

Freeze the cheesecake for 1 hour.

Once it has set, remove it from the tin, top with the sliced mango, pour the blended mango over the top and serve.

Notes:

CANNED COCONUT CREAM needs to be shaken well before measuring the 1/4 cup you need.

SOAK THE CASHEWS for a few hours, if you wish to (and discard the soaking water). But a good quality high powered blender or food processor should give a smooth, velvety consistency without soaking.

SERVES 8–10

1 1/2 cups macadamias or cashews, soaked in cold water for 1 hour

juice of 1 lemon (or more if you like a tartier tart!)

1 tablespoon agave syrup

2 tablespoons maple syrup

1/4 cup coconut butter (creamed coconut)

1 tablespoon coconut sugar

seasonal fresh fruit, e.g. blackberries, strawberries, banana, kiwi fruit, to serve

BASE

1 cup almonds

2 cups cashews

10 medjool dates, stoned

4 tablespoons unhulled tahini

CARAMEL SAUCE

1 cup medjool dates, stoned

1 cup cashews, soaked in cold water for 1 hour

1/3 cup coconut oil

1/2 cup maple syrup

RAW CREAMY DREAMY FRUIT FLAN

Want to win a dessert war? Make this flan! Creamy, dreamy and utterly irresistible, it took out the people's choice award in the Tastes of Central Geelong Dessert Wars, and is our most popular sweet treat.

FOR THE BASE, pulse the almonds, cashews, dates and tahini with 2 tablespoons water in a food processor until coarse and grainy (the mixture should stick together when pinched). Depending on size of food processor, base mix may have to be processed in two batches. When all base ingredients have been processed, press into a 25 cm loose-based flan tin. Cover with tea towel and place in the fridge while you make the filling.

FOR THE FILLING, place all the ingredients in a high-speed blender with 1/2 cup water and blend until smooth and creamy, scraping down the sides occasionally. To achieve a really creamy consistency a high-speed blender is required (Vitamix or Robot Coupe are winners from our experience). If you don't have a high-speed blender you can still achieve good results in a food processor – it will just take a bit longer and won't be quite as creamy.

Fill the flan tin with the filling mixture and refrigerate until firm, approximately 2 hours. Pop it in the freezer if you are in a hurry.

FOR THE SAUCE, blend all the ingredients with 1/3 cup of water in a high-speed blender until smooth, adding more water if the sauce is too thick. Keep blending until the sauce is warm. The sauce will warm with the heat from the blender motor. No further heating is required.

TO FINISH, when the flan is firm, cut into the desired number of slices before arranging the fresh fruit on top, then remove from tin. Be creative with your design – make a statement!

Carefully transfer slices of tart to serving plates, pour caramel sauce over the top and serve immediately.

Notes:

FOR A VERY WARM SAUCE we recommend sitting sauce in a container in a pot of boiling water. This will keep the temperature below 40°C so it is still considered raw.

COCONUT BUTTER is made from coconut flesh that has been ground to the consistency of very firm peanut butter, and can be found in health food stores.

WARM OREO BROWNIE WITH HOT CHOCOLATE SAUCE

SERVES 6

2 tablespoons sunflower oil

100 g Lindt Couverture Dark Chocolate

65 g self-raising flour

2 teaspoons cocoa powder

70 g caster sugar

pinch of Murray River pink salt (or sea salt)

2 teaspoons vanilla extract

90 ml soy milk

10 Oreo biscuits (plus extra for serving)

10 pistachios

HOT CHOCOLATE SAUCE

400 ml coconut milk

1/3 cup cocoa powder

1/3 cup caster sugar

30 g Lindt Couverture Dark Chocolate

We set out to create a dairy-free dessert that incorporated vegan cult favorites Oreos and Lindt dark chocolate. We did it – even avid milk chocolate lovers can't get enough of this indulgent treat. Happy baking!

Preheat oven to 140°C.

FOR THE BROWNIE, grease a square or rectangular baking tin with the oil and line with baking paper. The tin should be around 15–20 cm long.

Place chocolate into a heatproof bowl on top of a saucepan of gently simmering water, making sure the base of the bowl doesn't touch the water. Stir occasionally until chocolate is melted, then set aside.

Sieve the flour and cocoa powder into a large bowl, making sure they're combined evenly. Add the sugar, salt, vanilla extract, oil, soy milk and melted chocolate and stir using a whisk until smooth.

Roughly crush half the Oreos and fold through the mixture. Pour into prepared tin, using a soft silicone spatula to spread the mixture evenly.

Bake for 25–30 minutes. To ensure the brownie is cooked but still moist, check with a skewer every 2–3 minutes. When only a small amount of mixture sticks to the skewer, take it out of the oven. Place on a wire cooling rack for 5 minutes.

WARM OREO BROWNIE WITH HOT CHOCOLATE SAUCE

FOR THE CHOCOLATE SAUCE, put the coconut milk, cocoa powder, sugar and chocolate in a medium saucepan. Stir over low heat for 10 minutes.

Using a knife, finely crush the pistachios and remaining Oreos. Combine and set aside.

To serve, cut the brownie into thick rectangular slices and place on plates that will catch the chocolate sauce. Pour the hot chocolate sauce over and crumble the pistachio and Oreo mix on top. Cut Oreos in half and stick both halves into the top of each slice. Serve with a generous scoop of your favourite dairy-free ice-cream. Dust lightly with icing sugar.

Notes:

THE LINDT CHOCOLATE is available through The Source Bulk Foods.

OUR FAVOURITE VEGAN ICE-CREAM is Zebra Dream Vanilla Coconut Icecream.

WARM MEXICAN CORN & BLUEBERRY PUDDINGS

SERVES 4–6

PUDDINGS

300 g (2 cups) plain flour

110 g (3/4 cup) fine polenta

1 teaspoon salt

165 g (3/4 cup) brown sugar

170 g (3/4 cup) caster sugar

1 1/2 teaspoons baking powder

250 ml (1 cup) soy milk

60 ml (1/4 cup) vegetable oil

60 ml (1/4 cup) olive oil

1 teaspoon vanilla essence

zest and juice of 1 lemon

150 g blueberries, fresh or frozen

olive oil spray

BLUEBERRY TOPPING – see next page

Using corn chips in a crumble – let's just put it down to our head chef Shannon's weirdo brain. Sometimes, you can't question the ingenuity, especially when it tastes this good. These puddings are extra great served with a scoop of dairy-free vanilla ice-cream.

Preheat the oven to 170°C.

TO MAKE THE PUDDINGS place the flour, polenta, salt, both sugars and baking powder in the bowl of a stand mixer with a paddle attachment and mix for 10 seconds to evenly blend the ingredients.

Put the soy milk, both oils, vanilla and the lemon zest and juice in a jug and stir to combine.

With the motor running on low speed, pour in the wet ingredients then turn up to a medium speed and mix for 1 minute. Fold through the blueberries.

TO MAKE THE TOPPING, combine the blueberries, cornflour and caster sugar in a bowl and toss the mixture until the blueberries are well coated.

Spray a large 6-hole muffin tin with olive oil spray and place a small circle of baking paper in the base of each hole. Spoon a little of the blueberry topping into each hole then top with 2–3 heaped tablespoons of the muffin mixture. You can make smaller/more muffins if you prefer – just

WARM MEXICAN CORN & BLUEBERRY PUDDINGS

BLUEBERRY TOPPING

150 g blueberries, fresh or frozen

2 tablespoons cornflour

2 tablespoons caster sugar

CORN CHIP CRUMBLE

2–3 corn chips, crumbled

3 tablespoons polenta

65 g desiccated coconut

2 tablespoons brown sugar

pinch of ground cinnamon

2 tablespoons plain flour

pinch of salt

2 tablespoons melted butter

BLUEBERRY & LEMON SAUCE

155 g blueberries, fresh or frozen

110 g (1/2 cup) caster sugar

1/4 teaspoon ground cinnamon

juice and zest of 1 lemon

1/2 teaspoon vanilla essence

reduce the number of blueberries in the bottom slightly and adjust the cooking time.

Bake in the oven for 25–30 minutes or until a skewer inserted into the centre of a muffin comes out clean.

TO MAKE THE CORN CHIP CRUMBLE, place all of the ingredients in a mixing bowl and rub the mixture through your hands until everything is coated in the melted butter and well combined. Spread the mixture evenly onto a baking tray and bake for 20 minutes or until golden brown. Set aside to cool to room temperature, then break it into crumble-sized pieces, although keep the texture a little rough.

TO MAKE THE BLUEBERRY AND LEMON SAUCE, place all of the ingredients in a small saucepan and bring to a gentle simmer. Cook until the sugar is dissolved, then pour into a blender and blend until smooth.

Once the muffins are cooked, remove from the oven and place a chopping board or tray on top of the muffin tin, gently pressing down to flatten the cakes. Allow the muffins to cool for 5 minutes in the tin before inverting onto a wire rack.

Spoon a little of the sauce onto the base of each serving plate and place a pudding on top. Drizzle with a little extra sauce, then scatter the crumble mix over the plates.

This is an edited extract from Smith & Daughters: A Cookbook (that happens to be vegan) *by Shannon Martinez and Mo Wyse, published by Hardie Grant Books RRP $48.00 and available in stores nationally.*

RHUBARB & APPLE CRUMBLE

SERVES 12

2 kg apples (we use Golden Delicious)

1 bunch rhubarb

2 cups brown sugar

2 cups plain flour

3 cups rolled oats

5 cups cornflakes

2 cups desiccated coconut

400 g Nuttelex

vegan coconut ice-cream, to serve

This recipe is an old-school favourite. Growing up, we had a giant vegie garden in the backyard and rhubarb was always the star. This recipe is super easy and beyond yum! Make a big batch – some for now and some for later. Freeze the fruit and crumble separately.

Preheat oven to 180°C.

Peel and dice apples into approx. 2 cm chunks.

Remove leaves and ends of rhubarb, wash well, then chop into chunks the same size as the apples.

Place apples and rhubarb into a pot with 1 cup water and 6 teaspoons of the brown sugar. Mix well.

Simmer for 10 minutes until apples are soft.

Place the stewed fruit into two baking dishes.

FOR THE CRUMBLE, in a large bowl combine the flour, oats, coconut and remaining sugar and mix well.

Use your hands to mix in the Nuttelex until the mixture is crumbly, then mix in the cornflakes.

Sprinkle the crumble over the fruit and bake for 25 minutes or until starting to brown.

Serve warm with vegan coconut ice-cream.

Notes:

ANY FRUIT can be substituted for the rhubarb. Try apricots, plums, berries or whatever is in season.

PEAR UPSIDE-DOWN PUDDING

SERVES 6–8

6 canned pear halves

125 g plain flour

1/2 teaspoon bicarbonate of soda

pinch of salt

1 teaspoon ground ginger

1/4 teaspoon ground nutmeg

1/4 teaspoon ground cinnamon

egg replacer equivalent of 1 egg

125 g brown sugar

90 g golden syrup

1/2 cup soy milk

60 g vegan margarine or butter, melted

vegan cream or ice-cream, to serve

TOPPING

60 g vegan margarine or butter

100 g brown sugar

Here's a great upside-down pudding that my mum used to make and that I've veganised. To me, this recipe is proof that being vegan isn't hard – there are plenty of products that are readily available to make this dessert not only delicious but cruelty-free.

Preheat the oven to 180°C. Grease and line a 19-centimetre cake tin (not springform).

For the topping, melt the margarine in a small saucepan over low heat. Add the brown sugar and stir until melted.

Pour mixture into cake tin, then arrange pears over the base, cut side down.

In a large mixing bowl, sift together the flour, bicarbonate of soda, salt and spices.

In another bowl, beat the egg replacer, brown sugar, golden syrup, soy milk and melted margarine until well combined. Stir in the flour mixture and mix well.

Pour pudding batter over pears and bake for 40–45 minutes. Pudding is ready when a knife inserted into the centre comes out clean.

Cool in the tin for 10 minutes before turning out. Serve with vegan cream or ice-cream.

PUMPKIN PIE

SERVES 10–12

3 2/3 cups unsweetened canned pumpkin (see note)

1 1/4 cup coconut milk

1 cup sugar

1/4 cup cornstarch (see note)

2 teaspoon vanilla essence

1/2 teaspoon salt

1 teaspoon ground cinnamon

1/2 teaspoon ground ginger

1/4 teaspoon ground nutmeg

1/4 teaspoon ground cloves

PIE CRUST

1 3/4 cups unbleached all-purpose flour

1 teaspoon salt

1/2 cup vegetable, canola or other flavour-neutral oil

1/3 cup iced water

This is one of my favourite recipes: it's a sweet pie that I grew up on in America. It reminds me of many years of Thanksgiving and Christmas dinners at my grandmother's house, and of the good old days when something as simple as a slice of pie was all you needed to be happy. The cloves, ginger and nutmeg make this pie the epitome of comfort. The cinnamon is awesome as well, of course, but it's those three spices that really make it stand out. I hope this recipe brings you and your family many happy memories!

FOR THE PIE CRUST, combine the flour, salt and oil in a medium bowl and mix together until little pebbles form.

Add 1 tablespoonful of cold water at a time, mixing in between each addition until all combined. You want the mixture to form a nice, moist, pliable dough when pressed together. If too wet and sticky, or too dry and cracking, adjust with extra flour or water.

Form dough into a ball and roll it out between two pieces of baking paper or plastic wrap, or on a lightly floured surface. Flip it over into a 23 cm pie tin and press it into the tin with your fingers, making sure it's nice and snug in all the tight spaces. (If you don't have a rolling pin, you can just form the dough into a disc and press it into the pie tin.) The crust does not need to be pre-baked, so set aside while you prepare the filling.

FOR THE FILLING, preheat the oven to 180°C.

Combine the cooked pumpkin, coconut milk, sugar, cornstarch, vanilla, salt and spices in a medium bowl and mix by hand or using a hand mixer until completely combined and smooth.

Pour this mixture into your pie crust and level out the top. Bake on the middle rack of your oven for 1 hour and 20 minutes. If you have a digital kitchen thermometer, check that the temperature in the middle of the pie has reached 100°C (that's when cornstarch sets); otherwise, give the pie a gentle shake – it should jiggle just slightly in the centre when ready.

Cool pie on the bench for an hour then place in the fridge for a few hours.

Pie is best served cold or at room temperature, with a dollop of your favourite dairy-free whipped cream.

Notes:

CANNED PUMPKIN can be hard to find (and expensive) in Australia. To cook your own for this recipe, use butternut pumpkin for best results. Cut in half, wrap each half in foil and roast for up to an hour until soft. Scrape flesh from skin and puree. If it's watery, discard the liquid.

FOR THE PUREE, you will need about 2 kg butternut pumpkin to yield approximately 4 cups of puree. If you end up with too much puree, freeze the excess.

CORNSTARCH is cornflour made from 100 per cent corn, which has greater setting power. Check the ingredients when buying cornflour as it can be wheat-based. Use potato starch if allergic.

JESSICA BAILEY

Founder and director, The Cruelty Free Shop

Jessica Bailey started The Cruelty Free Shop in January 2001 as an online store, well before online stores were a thing. She had been vegan for about a year, and her biggest challenge was finding products she wanted to eat. She knew they were available overseas and figured that other people must be in the same position so she started importing some hard-to-get items. For the first five or six years it was a hobby that she ran from home. Now The Cruelty Free Shop stocks the biggest range of vegan products in Australia with stores in Sydney, Melbourne, Brisbane and Canberra, as well as online.

Jessica hadn't thought to question what went on in animal agriculture and the dairy industry until someone handed her a leaflet at the Newtown Festival in Sydney. 'It was about pigs, I think. I read it on the train on the way home and it opened up a whole world. I was pretty horrified by what I read. I contacted Animal Liberation and started volunteering, running stalls for fundraising.

'When I first became vegan, I heard people saying "I used to be vegan but it was just too hard." I wanted to make it easier for people to be vegan – or vegetarian – so they had no excuse not to be,' Jessica explains. Initially, gelatin-free lollies and dairy-free chocolate were in demand. 'You couldn't get anything like that back then,' Jessica says, noting how far things have come since she became vegan in 2000.

'Becoming vegan wasn't an overnight thing. I did what most people do: I dropped each different type of dead animal then finally dropped dairy. It was quite a

Jessica and Annabelle

progression over a long period of time – I think most of us make the change gradually,' she says.

Apart from sourcing food, Jessica's biggest personal challenge was dealing with other people's attitudes. 'When you say you're vegan, some people can feel a little bit threatened – you're not questioning them, but I think by virtue of just being vegan, they're forced to confront some things they really don't want to know about. I just try to be Joe Average, a happy friendly healthy person, and bust the stereotype that all vegans are hippies with alternative views. I want to send a message that we're just normal people.'

It's a business, of course, but the shop is a great vehicle through which Jessica can make change and educate people by connecting with the vegan community as well as a broader audience. She's the founder of The Cruelty Free Festival and Vegan Day Out.

'People have a set of barriers between themselves and making an ethical decision. Most people don't like to be different, they like to be part of a herd, but now that being vegan has become socially acceptable, another barrier has been broken down.'

'Being vegan is not hard, despite what anyone might say. It's a simple thing that has such an enormous impact, for animals, for the environment and for your health. Everyone benefits when you become vegan.'

HANDY THINGS

sauces
dressings
spreads

Every good vegan cook has a range of tasty tricks up their sleeve, multi-purpose sauces that add value to leftovers, zing to a sandwich or a salad, double as dips with vegie sticks, crackers or chips, or become simple pasta sauces. A sweet sauce on hand means you can produce dessert out of nowhere. Many of the recipes in this book include great sauces, dressings and spreads that can be used in many different ways. We've included some of them here – sweet and savoury – so you have a handy reference when your meal needs a little spicing up or you fancy a sweet treat. Use your imagination, work out your favourites and have your own jar of magic waiting in the fridge.

SAVOURY

TWO CHAPS	PAGE 26

GREEN GODDESS SAUCE

15 g parsley leaves, 15 g chives, 10 g mint leaves, 10 g tarragon leaves, 15 g Dijon mustard, 1 small clove garlic, 15 ml lemon juice, 120 ml soy milk, 1/2 teaspoon salt (or to taste) pinch of freshly ground white pepper, 130 ml mild olive oil, 20 g thick coconut yoghurt, optional

Place everything except the olive oil and coconut yoghurt into the bowl attachment of a stick blender. Blend until the herbs are chopped, then start adding the oil in a slow steady stream until it's emulsified and the herbs are finely blitzed. Add the yoghurt, if using, and mix with a spoon.

GALA'S ORGANIC KITCHEN	PAGE 71

GREEN TAHINI DIP

1/2 cup hulled tahini, 1/4 cup lemon juice, 2 tablespoons apple cider vinegar, 1–2 cloves garlic, chopped, 1/2 teaspoon salt, 1 cup parsley leaves, chopped

Place all the ingredients in a blender and blend with ½–1 cup of water to achieve the desired consistency. The dip will keep for 4–5 days in an airtight container in the fridge, and freezes well too. Coriander and mint work well too.

CORIANDER CASHEW CREAM

1 cup raw cashews, soaked for at least 5 hours, juice of 1 lemon, 1 tablespoon apple cider vinegar, large handful coriander, stalks and leaves roughly chopped, 1 teaspoon salt

Rinse and drain the cashews, then place in a blender with the remaining ingredients and 2/3 cup cold water. Blend on medium speed for a few minutes until smooth. Add a little more water if you prefer a slightly thinner cream. Note that you can use broken cashew pieces, which only have to be soaked for 1 hour.

CREAMY CORIANDER & LIME DRESSING

225 g silken tofu, 1/2 bunch coriander (washed super well), 1/8 teaspoon crushed garlic, juice of 1 lime, salt, to taste

Blend all the ingredients in a blender or stick blender for about 2–3 minutes, making sure there are no lumps. Store in an airtight container in the fridge for up to a week.

CHUNKY PESTO

1 bunch basil, large handful of rocket, 1–1 1/2 cups oil of your choice, juice of 1 lemon, crushed garlic (to taste), salt and pepper, 4 cups almonds

Place the basil, rocket, 1 cup oil, lemon juice, garlic, and salt and pepper to taste in the bowl of a food processor and process until smooth. Add the almonds and extra oil if you think it needs it, and pulse until only just chopped up. Check the salt, garlic, lemon and oil levels, stirring in any additions by hand.

SUPERGREEN PESTO

90 g pepitas, 1 teaspoon finely chopped garlic, 1 small bunch of kale, roughly chopped, 2 handfuls of baby spinach leaves, 1 bunch basil, leaves picked, juice of 1 lemon, 100 ml extra virgin olive oil, plus extra to adjust consistency, if needed, 1 teaspoon salt

Process the pepitas and garlic in a food processor, followed by the kale, spinach, basil, lemon juice and salt. Gradually pour in the olive oil, adding more if necessary until the pesto reaches an easily spreadable consistency. Season with the salt.

VGF BURGERS PAGE 80

APPLE CIDER VINAIGRETTE

1/3 cup extra virgin olive oil, 1/4 cup raw apple cider vinegar, 2 tablespoons fresh lemon juice, 1 tablespoon Dijon mustard, 1 to 2 tablespoons maple syrup (to taste), salt and pepper

Combine all the ingredients in a clean screw-top jar and shake until smooth. Taste and adjust the sweetness and seasoning as required.

CHARLIE'S RAW SQUEEZE PAGE 98

PEANUT DRESSING

200 g peanut butter, 1/4 cup tamari, 30 ml sesame oil, 30 ml lime juice, 1 1/2 tablespoons rice malt syrup, 2.5 cm piece of ginger, 1 clove garlic, pinch of cayenne pepper

Blend all the ingredients and 30 ml water in a blender for 2 minutes until smooth.

THE FOX HOTEL PAGE 151

CHIPOTLE AIOLI

1 small jar of your favourite vegan mayonnaise, chipotle paste (to taste), crushed garlic (to taste), salt and pepper

Mix all the ingredients together, tasting as you go to get the right balance of heat from the chipotle paste and garlic.

VGF BURGERS PAGE 48

TOFU AIOLI

250 g silken tofu, 1 clove garlic (or to taste), 1 teaspoon salt, pinch of cayenne pepper, juice of 1/2 a lemon

Blitz all the ingredients in a high-speed or bullet blender. Store in a sealed container in the fridge until required. Store in the fridge for up to 4 days.

SEE ALSO: Homemade Hummus (Anna Weatherlake, page 44), Creamy Chipotle Aioli (Elixiba, page 46), Lemon and Mint Yoghurt Dipping Sauce (Wombat Cafe and Store, page 52), Satay Sauce (Woking Amazing, page 56), Tahini and Miso Paste (Pollen 185, page 82), Goji and Ginger Dressing (The Little Shop of Plenty, page 92), Thai Dressing & Marinade (Woking Amazing, page 93), Miso, rice vinegar and tamari dressing (Transformer, page 96), Truffled Miso Aioli (Vegie Bar, page 106)

SWEET

BUKU CAKERY   PAGE 178

RASPBERRY CHIA COULIS

240 g frozen raspberries (thawed), 1 tablespoon rice malt or coconut syrup, 25 g chia seeds

Place all the ingredients in a bowl and mix gently. Refrigerate for at least 20 minutes before using.

WOMBAT CAFE AND STORE   PAGE 36

BERRY COMPOTE

500 g frozen berries (we use strawberries and blueberries)

Place the frozen berries in a saucepan and cook over low heat until heated through and softened. Simple! Keep in a sealed container in the fridge for up to five days.

DOLLY'S SISTER VEGAN CAFE & BAR   PAGE 190

CARAMEL SAUCE

1 cup medjool dates (stoned), 1 cup cashews (soaked in cold water for 1 hour), 1/3 cup coconut oil, 1/2 cup maple syrup

Blend all the ingredients with 1/3 cup water in a high-speed blender until smooth, adding more water if the sauce is too thick. Keep blending until the sauce is warm. For a very warm sauce, we recommend sitting sauce in a container in a pot of boiling water. This will keep the temperature below 40°C so it is still considered raw.

MATCHA MYLKBAR   PAGE 169

CHOCOLATE SAUCE

400 g Callebaut 74% dark chocolate, 200 ml full-fat coconut milk), pinch of salt

Melt the chocolate over a double boiler. In a separate pot, bring the coconut milk to a simmer. Slowly add the milk to the chocolate. When combined, add the salt. If you want an extra choc hit, we recommend adding a tablespoon of Mork dark cacao powder.

SEE ALSO: Coconut Cream (The Green Lion, page 186), Hot Chocolate Sauce (Small Print Pizza Bar, page 193), Blueberry & Lemon sauce (Smith & Daughters, page 195).

THANK YOU

This book you hold between your hands would never have seen the light of day without the talent and generosity of so many amazing people believing it would actually happen. So here's how we did it ...

INGREDIENTS

49 inspirational chefs (see page 213 for their details)

1 forever patient and to-die-for publishing consultant (Andrea McNamara)

1 astute chief nagger from Budapest (Andrea Davison)

1 diligent recipe editor (Sonja Heijn)

1 stellar food photographer (Julie Renouf)

1 amazing food preparation artist (Caroline Griffiths)

1 innovator for making food and everything else look fab (Lee Blaylock)

3 awesome models
(Bridie Goold, Ginevra Wright and Sophie Bazzano)

1 talented book designer (Karen Wallis)

2 crazy brave people from Affirm Press
(Martin Hughes and Keiran Rogers)

1 quirky South African and Edgar's Mission devotee (Kyle Behrend)

1 incredible and eagle-eyed lovely (Kerry Chaplin)

1 quick-witted and sharp-of-tongue foodie (Marieke Hardy)

1 inspirational and successful vegan business woman (Jessica Bailey)

1 musician who cast a line of kindness that transformed his life (Dan Maio)

1 kind cook (Melanie Baker)

1 hip couple who can never do enough for animals (Anna Weatherlake and Peter Siddle)

1 dairy that is not a dairy, only Half (a) Pint (Jules and Sam)

METHOD

Toss the above in a bowl of kindness, add a healthy splash of cruelty free fare and mix lovingly with all of my thanks and love.

Bake together for 12 months.

And voila! *Cooking with Kindness*, 240 pages that make being vegan easy!

If we could live happy and healthy lives without harming others ... why wouldn't we?

Pam Ahern

DIRECTORY

RECIPE CONTRIBUTORS

CAFES, RESTAURANTS, FOOD TRUCKS

RETAILERS & SUPPLIERS

COOKS

THE ALLEY

417 St Kilda Rd,

Melbourne VIC 3004

(03) 9820 8314

The Alley is a 35-seat venue on a mission to prove that plant-based eating doesn't mean you have to miss out on taste. They serve 100 per cent crave-able vegan food that everyone loves – vegans, paleo, celiac and meat-eaters alike – and their menu boasts signature house-made burgers, gluten-free pastas, seasonal soups, salads, cold-pressed juices, vegan ice cream and baked sweets like you've never seen them before.

Photo credit Jesse Thompson

thealley.net.au

BUKU CAKERY

555 High Street

Northcote VIC 3070

(03) 9481 6141

Specialising in delicious creations inspired by Mother Nature for gluten intolerance, lactose intolerance, vegans and vegetarians that are also free of refined sugar. Buku Cakery serves a daily variety of cakes and sweet treats, juices, smoothies, mylkshakes, coffee and a selection of teas; as well as light breakfast and lunch options.

buku.com.au

BURCH & PURCHESE SWEET STUDIO

647 Chapel Street

South Yarra VIC 3141

(03) 9827 7060

Chef Darren Purchese produces exquisite and extravagant sweet creations, skilfully balancing flavour and texture and combining delicious components to create works of sweet art. We always stock a vegan product in our daily fresh range of cakes & desserts. We also have a larger selection of vegan products in our non-perishable range including chocolate bars, jams and freeze dried fruit lollipops.

Photo credit: Ari Hatzis

burchandpurchese.com

CHARLIE'S RAW SQUEEZE

Various locations

With more than ten locations across Queensland, Charlie's Raw Squeeze is a revolutionary juice bar dishing up vegan offerings with plenty of raw, gluten-free, dairy-free and refined sugar-free options. For those seeking something more substantial these guys also run Brisbane's first dedicated vegan burger bar, Moo-free burgers.

rawsqueeze.com.au

THE CRUELTY FREE SHOP

Various locations across Australia

The Cruelty Free Shop is Australia's favourite purveyor of everything vegan, bringing you the widest range of vegan products including food, health, fashion, beauty, and household items. The shop was born with one simple mission: to make it easier for people to become and stay vegan. It's a haven for vegans, who can shop easily knowing someone's done the label reading for them.

crueltyfreeshop.com.au

DOLLY'S SISTER VEGAN CAFE & BAR

221 Moorabool St

Geelong VIC 3220

(03) 4245 1013

Dolly's Sister Vegan Cafe and Bar is the result of the amazing reception by the public of Simply Vegan Cuisine's Dolly Bus – Australia's first fully vegan mobile food van. Owners Steve and Lisa are passionate vegans who believe that food should be kind, compassionate, sustainable, healthy and incredibly tasty. Dolly Bus and Dolly's Sister serve delicious, hot, hearty home-cooked meals and amazing raw living dishes.

dollyssister.com.au

ELIXIBA

Maroochydore QLD

Robina QLD

Byron Bay NSW

Elixiba is a health-oriented venue where good times and good food come together. Based on the philosophy that you can enjoy a great night out that your body will thank you for the next day, they serve exquisite food and drinks infused with a variety of rare and wonderful active botanicals. They are a totally gluten-free venue.

elixiba.com

THE FOX HOTEL

351 Wellington St

Collingwood VIC 3066

(03) 9416 4957

This cunningly versatile pub turned modern eatery in Collingwood has a relaxed, welcoming vibe. The comprehensive food menu ensures vegans are never overlooked and the dedicated list of vegan-friendly beers and wines means your entire night is taken care of with ease.

thefoxhotel.com.au

GALA'S ORGANIC KITCHEN

Healthy and delicious, organic, vegan and gluten-free catering services in and around Sydney. Gala's Organic Kitchen offers catering for all kinds of retreats and workshops. Maria Carin runs cooking classes and demonstrations, works as a personal chef and is currently working on her first cookbook.

Photo credit: Darn Small

galasorganickitchen.com

GIGI PIZZERIA

379 King Street,

Newtown NSW 2042

Gigi is a proud member of the AVPN (the 'Associazione Verace Pizza Napoletana' or 'True Neapolitan Pizza Association'), one of a very few pizzerias in Sydney that can claim the honour. They adhere to the AVPNs incredibly specific regulations, including hand-stretched dough, traditionally topped, and wood-fired pizza, Napoli style. They are also 100 per cent meat and dairy free.

Photo credit: Jessica Matino

gigipizzeria.com.au

GIRLS & BOYS

382 Brunswick Street

Fitzroy VIC 3065

(03) 9417 6766

From the team behind Vegie Bar and Transformer, this all-vegan take away dessert bar describes itself as 'a nostalgic ode to the Mr Whippy of our youth, serving super good vegan vibes'.

girlsandboysfitzroy.com

THE GREEN LION

726 Darling St

Rozelle NSW 2039

0424 115 466

The Green Lion is Australia's first vegan pub bistro. Pub classics like burgers, pizza and hotdogs get a plant-based make over here, and the beer and wine list is 100 per cent animal-free. It's a rare treat to be able to walk into a pub and order absolutely anything from the menu.

thegreenlion.com.au

HEAVEN RAW CAFÉ

26 Montreal Street

Fremantle WA 6160

0418 742 917

Heaven Raw Café has been a part of the community hub that is FERN (Fremantle Environmental Resource Network) and provides raw and vegan food and education that is affordable to everyone. Not to mention delicious! Raw food classes show you how to make all of their goodies at home! You can start with the Chocolate Goji Slice on page 162.

heavenisarawvegancafe.org

LENTIL AS ANYTHING

Various locations

Lentil as Anything's mantra is 'food without borders'. They run five restaurants and a catering service, each with its own story, its own culture, and its own cuisine. With a pay-what-you-think model and firm belief that everyone deserves a place at the table – it's no wonder this place is a bone fide institution.

lentilasanything.com

THE LITTLE SHOP OF PLENTY

217 Railway Parade

Maylands WA 6051

Plenty is a little business in Perth with the goal of helping folks achieve better health simply by eating better food. They serve nutritional food filled with life – plenty of satisfying plant-based dishes that contain plenty of protein, plenty of minerals and plenty of exciting flavours to keep you coming back for more.

littleshopofplenty.com

218

MACCARONI OSTERIA ITALIANA

201 Queens Pde

Clifton Hill VIC 3068

(03) 9077 0377

maccaroniosteria.com.au

Head chef at Maccaroni Osteria, Alessandra D'Angelo, moved to Melbourne from the history-rich, culture-filled Palermo and has been committed to bringing the flavours from the land of the sun to her new home ever since. This authentic Italian restaurant offers a two-page-long separate menu dedicated to delicious Italian vegan creations and offers one of the most generous vegan banquets in Australia.

MAHA

21 Bond St

Melbourne VIC 3000

(03) 9629 5900

maharestaurant.com.au

At Maha, Shane Delia and his team create playful and full flavoured Middle Eastern food like nothing you've tasted before. Their tailor-made vegan menu offers diners the same carefully balanced and thought-provoking dining experience as all of their menus. Changing seasonally to ensure the best quality Victorian produce is incorporated, the vegan menu is a true indulgence, whether you choose the 4, 5 or 6 course option.

MATCHA MYLKBAR

72A Acland St

St Kilda VIC 3182

(03) 9534 1111

matchamylkbar.com

Located on the bustling corner of Acland St and Carlisle St, Matcha Mylkbar injects a much-needed boost of #cleaneating creativity into the St Kilda food scene. The Matcha Mylkbar menu is entirely plant-based and has been carefully crafted to appeal to vegans, vegetarians, the dietary intolerant, the dietary ignorant and the dietary indifferent alike. The eponymous matcha is of course the drink of choice, featuring in many different forms across the menu.

MISTER NICE GUY'S BAKESHOP

151 Union Rd

Ascot Vale VIC 3032

0416 848 610

Mister Nice Guy's Bakeshop is your allergy friendly one stop shop. Everything in their bakery is 100% egg-free, dairy-free, lactose-free, cochineal and gelatine-free, with soy-free, gluten-free, wheat-free, corn-free, fructose-free and low GI options. They believe that anything you need in a recipe can be found in cruelty-free ways and made even better...

Photo credit: Marian Morgan

misterniceguy.com.au

MORRIS JONES & CO

163 Chapel St

Windsor VIC 3181

(03) 9533 2055

Head Chef Matthew Butcher's style of food is original, quirky, fun contemporary Australian cuisine designed to complement their magnificent 1887 heritage building. Their four-course vegan tasting menu is Melbourne fine dining at its best.

morrisjones.com.au

MR BLACK JUICERY

1 Blackburne Square

Berwick VIC 3806

(03) 9707 5143

A whole food, plant based cafe, Mr. Black Juicery focuses on creating wholesome nutritious food that tastes delicious and nourishes from the inside out. Passionate about helping others adopt a healthy lifestyle, all their food is made from scratch, is completely vegan, gluten-free and free of refined sugar, in line with the philosophy of its founders who live this lifestyle every single day.

mrblackjuicery.com.au

NOSTRALIS WHOLEMEAL, VEGETARIAN & VEGAN PIZZA

55 Hawthorn Rd

North Caufield VIC 3161

(03) 9528 4961

nostralis.com

Nostralis has been serving delicious wholemeal vegetarian pizza since 1981. Their bases are made with 100 per cent organic wholemeal flour and they pride themselves on only using the freshest ingredients. The cheese they use is made with vegetable rennet, and they can offer (by request) 100 per cent soya cheese and gluten-free, wheat-free bases so vegans and coeliacs don't miss out. This is truly mouth-watering guilt-free pizza.

PANA CHOCOLATE

panachocolate.com

Pana Barbounis founded Pana Chocolate in Melbourne with the intention of creating a rich, luxurious chocolate the whole world could enjoy. Chocolate made from vegan, organic ingredients with no refined sugar, and produced using minimal heat (raw). Chocolate that loves what's within, as well as the earth it came from. For a taste of Pana, shop online, visit a Pana Chocolate Shop, and buy the cookbook.

POLLEN 185

4/183-185 King William Rd

Hyde Park SA 5061

Pollen 185 offers home-style cooking with influences from around the globe. Their food, is filling, colourful and full of love; designed to delight the eyes and soul. Their coffee is roasted locally, all wines are from regional SA and their hot sauces, chai, cacao sauce, almond brazil and cashew mylk all made in-house. There are many things that make this place your home away from home. Pollen is not about fads, but about flavour and vibe.

Photo credit: Lee Lam

pollen185.com.au

POWER PLANT

2-6 Swilk St

Templestowe VIC 3106

(03) 8838 1282

Power Plant is one of a kind in Melbourne's north east. The café offers vivid and nourishing 100% plant-based breakfasts and lunches both in a sunlit dining room and under a shaded balcony. The menu is confident, clever and underpinned by the defining idea that healthy, house-made food can be tempting and affordable, too.

powerplantcafe.com.au

THE RAW KITCHEN

181A High St

Fremantle WA 6160

(08) 9433 4647

The Raw Kitchen is proud to be Australia's largest dedicated plant-based restaurant. Set in an original 1920s warehouse and centred around an ethos of health and sustainability, The Raw Kitchen combines their plant-based restaurant with an eco retail store, yoga studio and event space. The menu showcases progressive raw and cooked plant-based dishes with a focus on quality, taste and innovation, all free from dairy, gluten and refined sugars.

therawkitchen.com.au

RED SPARROW

406 Smith St

Collingwood VIC 3066

(03) 94171454

Red Sparrow Pizza offers a modern and ethical twist on the classic pizzeria using the highest quality local and imported ingredients. Craft beers, fine wine and delicious wood fired pizzas are their thing, and they do all three very well (without an animal product in sight).

Photo credit: Love Bree Photography

redsparrowpizza.com

SEROTONIN EATERY

52 Madden Grove

Burnley VIC 3121

(03) 9528 8256

Serotonin Eatery is a plant-based cafe providing foods that encourage mood regulation. Their goal is to make you happy. All produce in this gorgeous café and event space is sourced from quality farmers, is organic where possible and has no BAD-itives. Even better, each dish on the menu contains all the colours of the rainbow – helping you increase your daily intake of fruits and vegetables.

serotonindealer.com

SMALL PRINT PIZZA BAR

388 High St

Windsor VIC 3181

(03) 9533 8402

Small Print is an eco-conscious, vegan-friendly pizzeria in Windsor. Their food philosophy is *local and organic* and they are committed to serving low-mileage food that is rich in flavour and full of the good stuff. Everything they can't make themselves comes from partners who share the same passion for sustainability and they aim to work in a closed loop: minimise waste, compost, recycle, reuse, then give back. Simple.

smallprintpizza.com.au

SMITH & DAUGHTERS

175 Brunswick St

Fitzroy VIC 3065

(03) 9939 3293

Smith & Daughters is the collaboration of two women with a strong commitment to bringing delicious food to the world. Their Latin-inspired cuisine highlights dishes from Mexico, Columbia, Peru, Spain and more: great coffee, sweets and a takeaway arm (Smith & Deli). All this without a single animal product on site. Truly plant-based, natural and organic when possible, Smith & Daughters are as compassionate as they are empowered.

Photo credit: Bonnie Savage

smithanddaughters.com

SOUL BURGER

Randwick, NSW 2031

(02) 9398 7496

Glebe, NSW 2037

(02) 9277 4624

Soul Burger is Australia's first gourmet plant-based burger joint. They want to launch a blitzkrieg on big agriculture and spark a shift in Aussie Food Culture towards plant-based foods. One visit and you'll be lusting after their plant-based beef burgers and addictive chips. Their coconut shakes will rock your world, and the whole experience will have you strung out between visits.

soulburger.com.au

STRAIGHT UP COFFEE AND FOOD

202 Liverpool St

Hobart TAS 7000

(03) 6236 9237

With a straight-up approach to food, this delightful cafe in Hobart provides clean-eating with a smile. Their menu is completely vegetarian and gluten-free and includes low- and no-refined-sugar deserts. To top it all off, they roast their own coffee and are open 7 days a week.

straightupcoffeeandfood.com.au

TRANSFORMER

99 Rose St

Fitzroy VIC 3065

(03) 9419 2022

Transformer serves up some of the most sophisticated vegan and vegetarian fare in Australia. Located in a beautifully revamped transformer factory with a gorgeous ivy-covered courtyard, the surrounds are almost as good as the creations you'll find on your plate.

transformerfitzroy.com

TWO CHAPS

122 Chapel St

Marrickville NSW 2204

(02) 9572 8858

Two Chaps is a produce-driven cafe by day with its own sourdough bakery and artisan pastry offering. On Thursdays and Fridays they're also open at night for fresh pasta. Everything on the menu is made from scratch in-house and it just so happens to be all vegetarian.

twochaps.com.au

URBAN PROJUICE

315 Montage Street

Albert Park VIC 3206

(03) 9696 0048

Urban Projuice is a wholefood cafe and juice bar in Albert Park run by a community of down-to-earth foodies dedicated to nourishing your body and satisfying your senses. They are committed to serving fresh produce that is locally grown, seasonal, fair-trade and organic where possible.

urbanprojuice.com.au

THE VEGAN DAIRY

The Vegan Dairy creates plant-based cheeses and butters that taste like the real thing. They are handcrafted with the finest, most nourishing ingredients. So whether you are vegan, lactose intolerant, health conscious, or simply want to share food with friends or family who are, you can enjoy guilt-free cheeses and butters! Buy online or check the website for stockists.

thevegandairy.com.au

VEGIE BAR

380 Brunswick St

Fitzroy VIC 3065

(03) 9417 6935

From humble beginnings over 20 years ago, Vegie Bar has grown to become one of Melbourne's most popular haunts for both the health conscious and the hungry. Serving a vast array of dishes inspired by the world over, Vegie Bar continues to treat the masses to delicious and accessible contemporary vegetarian cooking.

vegiebar.com.au

VEGILICIOUS

118 Carlisle Street

St Kilda VIC 3182

(03) 9537 3820

Vegilicious offers wholesome, vegetarian soul food incorporating the freshest ingredients with multicultural influences and a passion for food. Their menu combines seasonal specials with regular favourites offering vegan and gluten free options upon request. Meals are primarily delicious, but also colourful, generous and nutritious.

vegilicious.com.au

VGF BURGERS (JACK GUY FINE FOOD)

Jack Guy is a private-dining chef based in Melbourne. Working with fresh, simple, local seasonal ingredients, he will take care of all your dining needs so you can sit back and relax with your guests. He has recently launched VGF Burgers, which delivers 100 per cent vegan and gluten-free burgers across Melbourne, available through UberEats.

Photo credit: Brent Parker Jones

jackguyfood.com   vgfburgers.com

VON'S VEGAN BAKE HOUSE

Online orders and markets around Victoria

....

info@vonsveganbakehouse.com.au

....

vonsveganbakehouse.com.au

Von's Vegan Bake House is a boutique artisan bakery based in Melbourne. With locally sourced seasonal produce, Yvonne creates baked goods that are 100 per cent plant based and cruelty free. From her signature spongy lemon layer cake topped with lavender frosting, to fusion spun black sesame match blocks, from healthy nuts-and-seeds slice to the culinary icon, jam-filled lamingtons, her delicacies will not only satisfy your appetite, but leave you craving more.

WOKING AMAZING

0481 861 642

....

facebook.com/WokingAmazing   instagram.com/WokingAmazing

Woking Amazing is a 100 per cent vegan mobile food business. They provide Asian street food dishes with a twist and have become an absolute vegan institution. When they're not at one of Melbourne's dedicated food-truck parks, you can find them peddling their creations to excited customers at festivals all over Victoria. For all updates follow Woking Amazing on Facebook and Instagram.

WOMBAT CAFE & STORE

230 Boundary Road

....

Dromana VIC 3936

....

(03) 5987 1193

....

facebook.com/wombatcafeandstore

The Mornington Peninsula's first 100 per cent vegan cafe and store. Open 7 days a week serving locally roasted Little Rebel coffee, smoothies, breakfast and lunch. Try the range of house made cakes and treats including choc-coated honeycomb and their Wombat Balls. There's also a great range of grocery items, books and giftware.

Photo credit: lovethepen.com

INDEX

Text copyright © Pam Ahern, Edgar's Mission 2017
Recipe copyright © the contributors
Photographs © Julie Renouf 2017, except where otherwise specified

10 9 8 7 6 5 4 3

National Library of Australia Cataloguing-in-Publication entry available for this title at www.nla.gov.au

Title: Cooking with Kindness / Edgar's Mission and Pam Ahern, authors.
ISBN: 9781925584394 (paperback)

Cover and book design by Karen Wallis, Taloula Press
Cover image by Julie Renouf
Photography by Julie Renouf
Photographer's assistant: Linda Oliveri
Prop and food styling by Lee Blaylock
Food preparation by Caroline Griffiths
Project management by Andrea McNamara
Wardrobe styling models' own

Photographs on pages iv–v, 2, 41, 131 and 203 are by Kyle Behrend.
Models are Bridie Goold (pages 51, 53, 85, 105, 135, 185, 188), Ginevra Wright (pages 18, 39, 91,
cover) and Sophie Bazzano (pages 45 and 184).

Colour reproduction by Splitting Image Colour Studio, Clayton, Victoria
Printed in China by C&C Printing
Printed on FSC accredited paper stock